A PIECE OF CHANGE

Counting The Cost of True Transformation

Ifedayo Greenway
& 12 Transformational Writers Emerging from Their Cocoons

A PIECE OF CHANGE

Copyright © 2024 Ifedayo Greenway

All rights reserved.

No part of this book may be reproduced, distributed, or transmitted in any form by any means, graphic, electronic, or mechanical, including photocopy, recording, taping, or by any information storage or retrieval system, without permission in writing from the publisher, except in the case of reprints in the context of reviews, quotes or references.

Scripture quotations marked NLT are taken from the Holy Bible, New Living Translation Copyright © 1996, 2004, 2007, 2013, 2015 by Tyndale House Publishers Inc. Scripture quotations marked KJV are taken from the King James Version, Public domain. Scripture quotations marked MSG are taken from The Message Bible, Copyright © 1993, 1994, 1995, 1995, 1996, 2000, 2001, 2002 by Eugene H. Peterson. Scripture quotations are taken from The Holy Bible, New International Version® NIV® Copyright © 1973, 1978, 1984, 2011 by Biblica, Inc.™ Used by permission. All rights reserved worldwide

Printed in the United States of America

ISBN: 979-8-9868570-9-1

Ifedayo is available for speaking engagements, book signings, and workshops. Send your requests to
ifegreenway@igandmore.com

Special discounts are available on bulk quantity purchases by book clubs, associations and special interests groups. For more details email: ifegreenway@igandmore.com

To the butterflies,
Those who long for true transformation,
Who dare to break free from the cocoon,
And who are ready to embrace the true cost of their change journey.
May you soar boldly into the unknown,
Trusting that every tear, every trial, and every triumph
Is shaping you into the beautiful, resilient soul you were meant to be.
This is for you — the brave ones,
Who know that real change begins within

Contents

Introduction 1

What Are You Afraid of Butterfly? 4
   Ifedayo Greenway

Seasons Change 17
   Sonya the SheE.O

Healing Hatred 27
   Angela N. Jackson

The Heart Shift 37
   Mendy Huff

The Transforming Impact of Love, Faith,
   and Forgiveness 46
   Rev. Dr. Angela B. Jones

A Silent Apology 57
   Charmaigne L. Lloyd

No Longer Voiceless: My Cinderella Story 68
   Natasha Broughton

A Glimpse of Metamorphosis 76
   Leona Elzy

Independent Love 87
   Salesha LOL

My Reflection Unveiled 99
  Michelle M. Hicks

Trials, Thorns, and Triumphs 108
  Zaquinntia "Zee" Chamblee

Stepping Away from Safety 118
  Renita D. Harris

I'm Finally A Butterfly 130
  Princess Barnes

Fly Butterfly Fly 141

About The Authors... 143

Introduction

Welcome, dear reader. Before you embark on this journey of transformation, allow me to share a story from my perspective. I am the butterfly—a symbol of change, growth, and beauty. But I didn't begin this way. My wings were not always vibrant, nor was I always free to soar. My story, much like yours, began in the most humble and unassuming of places.

I started as an egg, so small you might overlook me, but inside, everything I would one day become was already present. The potential for transfiguration was there, waiting to unfold. In this stage, I had no idea of the beauty, pain, or challenges that lay ahead. I simply existed, cradled in stillness, preparing for the journey to come. Perhaps, you too, are in a season of quiet beginnings, where the whispers of change are just starting to echo in your heart.

Then came the moment I emerged as a caterpillar, driven by a deep thirst and hunger to grow. I consumed everything around me, feeding on knowledge, experiences, and new life lessons. Each leaf I devoured was like a step forward, a piece of the journey that would help me become something more. I felt awkward, unsure of what I was becoming, but I knew that growth was a mandate.

But there came a time when growth alone wasn't enough. I needed to retreat, to enter the chrysalis—a place of stillness, darkness, and true transformation. It was in this cocoon that the most miraculous and powerful changes occurred. I wasn't sure what would happen, but I had to trust the process, even though it felt like everything I knew was dissolving. I was becoming something new, even though I couldn't see the outcome yet. This was the hardest part of change: the letting go, the surrender to the unknown. If you're in this phase, I understand how uncomfortable it can be. But I promise you, the stillness is where God does His best work.

And then, one day, I emerged. Slowly, I stretched my wings, fragile at first but growing stronger with each fluttering movement. The process had been long, but here I was—a butterfly, transformed. I was no longer who I had been, but every stage of my journey was necessary to become who I was meant to be. My wings, now vibrant and full of life, carry me to new heights. This is the freedom that comes after embracing the true cost of transformation.

As you open the pages of this book, *A Piece of Change*, I invite you to step into your own metamorphosis. Each chapter offers personal stories, relatable challenges, insights, guidance, and reflections that will help you navigate the stages of your change journey. Just as the butterfly must undergo each stage to fully become what it was meant to be, you too will experience your own unique process of growth and emergence.

Transformation is not always easy, but it is always worth it. Embrace each stage, trust the process, and know that on the other side of your journey lies the beauty and freedom of your true self. Let this book be your companion as you discover the power and purpose in your own piece of change.

What Are You Afraid of Butterfly?

Ifedayo Greenway

~~~

By the time this book reaches your hands, and you start delving into this chapter, I'll be somewhere adjusting to my new life in an empty dwelling. Perhaps tears will still be lingering as I navigate one of the toughest parental transformations. This book is set for release shortly after my youngest child, my only daughter, heads off to college. My thoughts as I write this chapter sync with anxiety and heart palpitations and echo the question that ricocheted in my mind a million times in the past year: "What am I going to do when she leaves?"

I vividly remember the moment I found out the gender of my third child. The excitement was so overwhelming that I nearly fell off the examination table when my doctor announced, "It's a girl!" It was an unexpected, and if I'm honest - an unwanted pregnancy, yet it was an answer to a prayer. When I married my ex-husband, I had two sons, and he had no biological children. He accepted the boys as his own and seamlessly eased into being a stepfather; however, he prayed for a child of his own. I was so against the idea, but I figured if I had to take one for the team, the least God could do was give me a girl this time. I was delighted to be a boy mom, but they were giving me a run for my money. You hear me! Those boys were boy-ing, and I loved every tiring minute of it. From football fields to basketball courts, track and field events, and stage performances, I was deeply involved in their lives and determined to nurture their gifts and talents. One was my all-American athlete, and the other was my theater kid. I prided myself on being present at every game and musical theater moment. They also did all the other things that boys did. They brought bugs into the house to scare me, found trouble some days at school, took daredevil chances with their lives, fought each other a lot, and fought other people for each other. They lived by the old creed, "I can fight my sibling, but you better not touch him." One thing was clear, they were bonded as brothers but also had their own unique testament to the multifaceted journey of growing up as a male child. The boys were eleven and eight when my daughter was born. And boy (no pun intended…lol) did she bring a whole new energy into our home. Her presence softened the roughness of the boy's life, which had become our norm.

Sports-themed bathrooms gave way to pink, angelic murals on the walls, marking a shift in dynamics that I welcomed with open girl mom arms. As the only princess of the house, she was definitely doted on and coddled. She was the absolute apple of her daddy's eye, and her brothers were raised to protect her. Because of the age difference between my children, she spent years at home alone with me. She got to experience only-child perks when her brothers went off to the military and college. Despite being the epitome of a daddy's girl, she and I managed to develop a special bond, the kind of mother-daughter relationship I dreamed of. Throughout her childhood years, I'd kiss her and say, "You're my favorite girl," to which she'd always reply, "Mommy, I'm your only girl." Those exchanges rendered my heart as candle wax. I'd smile, and everything inside of me just melted.

When my daughter was eight, our lives took a forceful turn. We learned that her daddy, who by this time was my ex-husband, was terminally ill with Lou Gehrig's Disease, also known as ALS. The news infiltrated her little heart, causing unavoidable breakage. ALS is a progressive neurodegenerative disease that ultimately leads to paralysis and, in most cases, death within a few years of diagnosis. She knew all about it because, ironically, she had read the story of Lou Gehrig while in school. I remember her saying to me one day, "Mommy, I'm scared because Lough Gehrig died at the end of the story." As her father's health deteriorated, my daughter spent more and more time at his house. Although he was remarried, she shouldered responsibilities beyond her years, assuming caretaking roles and emotional burdens that no child should have to bear. Not because she was expected to, but because she wouldn't have it any other way. Her resilience during this challenging period was a testament to her strength and maturity. My daughter and I drew closer as we navigated the emotional turmoil and practical challenges of accepting our new reality. We shared our fears, sadness, and hopes for the future. Through her early teenage years, we became each other's confidants, providing comfort and reassurance during times of depleting hope. Our bond strengthened as we faced the uncertainties and the inevitable end of her father's illness together. On September 5, 2022, just one day before the start of her junior year in high school, her daddy peacefully drifted into his eternal healing. Grief snatched our lives away from us and penetrated our hearts in ways that I cannot describe. Our relationship evolved in ways that revealed both healthy and unhealthy aspects of co-dependency. The intensity of our shared grief sometimes blurred the boundaries of coping and healing. I found myself prioritizing my daughter's emotional needs over my own. Sometimes, prioritizing her pain gave me what I thought was a legitimate excuse not to face my own. And then there were days when she felt the need to become my caretaker. I had silently slipped into a dark place as life kept piling on challenges. This dynamic, while rooted in love and protection, occasionally hindered our ability to appropriately process grief independently. I was now her only parent. She needed her mommy, and I needed those nights of us sitting in the bed with pints of ice cream, sharing tear-jerking laughs, and watching game shows like two little old ladies. We were, and for all intents and purposes, still are, each other's healing place. I'm not saying every part of our journey was right or wrong - I'm saying that we gave our best effort to get through some very hard times.

The start of her senior year escorted in a new wave of emotions for me. I was excited that my girl was growing up and proud of her fight and tenacity to live beyond her daddy's death. But, I was also nervous, scared, and anxious about what this transition would mean for me individually. As we got closer to her prom, high school graduation, various momentous celebrations, graduation, and college send-off party, I cried a lot! Someone asked me if my tears were tears of joy. But honestly, there were days that I wasn't sure what my tears consisted of. I just knew I needed to cry and release whatever emotions they represented. I'm sure some were happy tears as these were major milestones that would make any parent elated, but I also know that some were filled with more grief and so many questions; "Who am I going to become when my last child leaves home?"

In the midst of my daughter's end-of-senior-year activities, I was also leading the charge as the visionary of this book collaboration. In a transformation training session with the writers, I talked about the power of authentically identifying the areas in our lives that require change. I likened the writing process to the stages of a butterfly. That night, the writers shared some deep intimate thoughts about their fears of releasing their stories. I led a few of them through my infamous *What Are You Afraid Of* coaching exercise as we peeled back the layers of fears that could potentially block us from telling our truths. What was meant to be a training moment for others quickly turned into a self-reflective moment that left me with perhaps one of the most daunting questions yet, "What are *YOU* afraid of, butterfly?" Resisting the rhetorical way of escaping the question, I was forced to come face-to-face with the answers in my own writing time.

I am afraid of being completely alone.

What if God never sends me anyone else to love me? As an empty nester, I am afraid of what empty means to me. I am scared witless of empty nest syndrome (the grief that many parents feel when their children move out of the home). I fear her departure will trigger the compounded extended grief disorder that my therapist once diagnosed me with. I am afraid of who and what God will expect me to become without the legitimate distraction of parenting to keep me from blossoming further into my purpose.

I'm 46 years old. I have been a parent for 29 of those years. One constant thing in my life, even when other relationships fell apart, was the presence of my children in the home. For many of those years, I was a single parent. Navigating through the victories and losses of single parenting was rewarding and draining. My kids became my reason. The reason I lived. The reason I pushed to heal after the divorce. The reason I worked so intentionally on building a career. The reason I didn't give up when life's challenges felt unbearably hard. The reason why my covenant with God was strengthened. With God's help, I thrived out of my cocoon as a parent. My wings were strong and colorful as I nurtured them through their own metamorphosis. My daughter leaving represents the last butterfly breaking the cocoon and soaring into adulthood. With three adult children, what does becoming a butterfly look like without the daily hands-on responsibility of being a mom? For me, the thought of going through a new transfiguration, re-entering the stages of change, and emerging as a woman in the second act of my life terrifies me. I'm frightened that this time, I will emerge from the cocoon as an unaccompanied, fragile, fluttering mess - my wings blanched and lacking the boldness of color I possessed as a parent. And my daughter won't be around to be the healing place we created.

I've studied the butterfly enough to know that it goes through four different life stages: egg stage, larva stage, pupa stage, and adult stage. In my last encounter with the study material, I remember asking myself a question. *Does it hurt to become a butterfly?* I researched to learn that although butterflies know when they are touched, their nervous system does not have receptors that register pain. However, for a caterpillar, metamorphosing into a butterfly is painful. So I ask myself again, "What are you afraid of, butterfly?" And my honest answer is, "I'm afraid of the pain of *this* metamorphic change."

One morning, I was reading. I was on day four of a seven-day devotional titled Dangerous Prayers by Pastor Craig Groeschel. Day four was entitled "Reveal My Fears" - *"Lord, reveal what holds my mind hostage. Show me what I fear the most. Go ahead, help me face what terrifies me".* Pastor

Groeschel explained that what we fear the most is the area where we trust God the least. What I fear the most shows where I need to grow with God. But the good thing is, as God reveals my fears, He will also rebuild my faith.

Wow! So, my anxious obsessing over being alone means that I don't trust God with the relationships in my life. While this was an illuminating moment, this is not a new fear for me. My trust meter has registered on the low end in this area before. In my previous book, *Removing The Fear,* I wrote, "Fear fed my twisted perception of a limited God and caused me to hold on to things and people far past their expiration date. I refused to accept good-byes, fought to hold on to the familiar, and justified dragging out-of-season things into new seasons."

I wrote that book in 2022, and here I am in 2024, dealing with the same fears. What was God trying to show me? Could it be that I have been dealing with the symptoms of my fears rather than the root causes? Symptoms are the visible indications of an issue (my tears and the physical indicators of anxiety), while root causes are the underlying, fundamental reasons behind it (my contaminated perspective and trust issues - the lies). It is vital to differentiate between the two because addressing symptoms alone is a short-term solution to the problem. This means the problem will continue to resurface after the Band-Aid that was on the indicators falls off. I had been addressing *how* I felt and not the real root cause of the *why.*

A child leaving for college is the natural progression of a parent letting go, so the question beyond the symptomatic display of my feelings is not what I am afraid of. Rather, it is why I am so afraid; what are the entrenched lies beneath the surface of all of these fears?

When I started writing this chapter, there were cracks in my foundation. My heart pumped lies that my mind believed and my mouth regurgitated: *God loves and will take care of everyone else except for me. God intentionally withholds things from me that He has the means to provide because He wants to see me suffer. God will always dangle joy and disappoint me at the end.* I did not trust God to take care of the people I love the most. I did not trust God to grace my life with the joy of having people who genuinely love me. For years, I have depended on the unconditional love of my children to fill a relational void. Years ago, I coined my daughter as #MyMiya. It was a cute little social media hashtag and name on the surface, but I now believe that the undertone was rooted in a territorial belief that no one (other than her daddy) could/would love her as I do. It was the belief that as my offspring, God would withhold from her what I told myself He was withholding from me - His love.

Back to the butterfly. I now understand that the stages of a butterfly represent stages of change and growth. There are stages of suffering, isolation, alone time (in the cocoon), and pain that we must go through to get to the place where we can spread our wings. The challenge of becoming a butterfly is twofold - learning to respect the process but also committing to unlearning anything contradictory to blossoming into destiny. This kind of life transition is not just about becoming; it's about unbecoming! I heard someone say that the butterfly has to unlearn its habit of crawling (being a caterpillar) if it's ever going to embrace its new wings. Therefore, I need to unlearn and detach myself from the rooted lies. Unlearn the contaminated perspective derived from wounded wings. Unbecome all of the things that the broken butterfly within me has taught me so that I can embrace the beauty of the new butterfly that I am becoming. But I'm also wise enough to know that unbecoming is not an immediate or easy feat.

So, what is this piece of change, you ask? I've been eagerly waiting to share it with you. The essence of change lies in the peace we will find throughout the process, trusting that something beautiful will emerge in the end. You are the stunning result of a profound transformation. Earlier in the chapter, I touched briefly on the stages of the butterfly. Now, let me provide more details to help you understand how both you and I will emerge as extraordinary manifestations of this powerful metamorphosis.

It begins humbly, with a single egg, a promise of what's to come, and the process in between. From this tiny vessel of life emerges a creature (you and I) filled with an insatiable hunger for more —the caterpillar. It devours, grows, and stretches beyond its limitations (through all of the pain), fueled by an inner fire guiding it toward who God created it to be.

As the caterpillar's journey progresses, a call to something greater takes hold of its soul, something unseen but deeply felt. It surrenders to this primal urge, wrapping itself in a cocoon of possibility, shedding the old and embracing the unknown.

Within the depths of this chrysalis, change unfolds. Things rearrange, dreams take flight, and the ordinary gives way to the extraordinary. In this sacred transformation space, the caterpillar dissolves into a soupy essence, shedding layers of its former self (the embedded lies) to reveal the essence of its true nature—a creature destined to fly.

Emerging from the depths of darkness, reborn and renewed, the butterfly unfolds its wings—a triumphant testament to the power of metamorphosis. No longer bound by earthly constraints, it soars skyward, a beacon of hope and inspiration.

In its graceful dance through life, the butterfly silently screams a universal truth—that within each of us lies the potential for profound transformation. Like the butterfly, we, too, can shed the shell of our past, embrace change, and emerge as the designers of our destiny we are. Whew! If that's not a chunk of change I don't know what is. But, perhaps the most exciting part of all of this is that I am not the only one with valuable coins of wisdom to offer. The upcoming chapters are also from other beautiful butterflies who were determined to go through the stages of growth and emerge from their cocoons. My prayer for you, my friend, is that as you read their stories, you will take *A Piece of Change* from each one until you have accumulated enough insight and motivation to cover the cost of your true transformation.

Oh! And to answer the question posed earlier in my chapter, "What am I going to do when she leaves"… I am going to fly butterfly fly!

In its graceful dance through life, the butterfly silently screams a universal truth—that within each of us lies the potential for profound transformation.

— **Ifedayo Greenway**

Seasons Change

Sonya the SheE.O

I lay there for as long as I could. My back was turned towards him, and the covers were pulled tightly over my head. My body felt heavy like an elephant had plopped down and refused to get off of me. My face was wet from the tears I tried to hide. I tried to lift my eyelids, but the emotions that consumed me wouldn't let me. I tossed and twisted until I finally felt the weight let up a little, just enough to stumble to my feet. My breathing got heavier, and all I could see was darkness in a room full of sunlight. In my mind, I screamed with all of my might, "Help me!" But in reality, my plea came out as a whisper.

At that moment, I felt the presence of God and the ancestors. I felt them usher my lifeless body into my bathroom, where I closed the door, stripped naked, and turned on the shower. I had just enough strength to step in and drop to my knees. I cried. I wailed. I broke. I realized that it was time to walk away from the man I trusted with my heart. My marriage was over, and my heart was torn to pieces. Words of apology poured from my mouth like a fountain. I felt the embrace of the ancestors as God filled me with His grace and mercy. The water felt like bricks rolling off my back. My rebirth had begun.

A Piece Of Change

I rose with my head held high. I heard God's words clear as day, "Now go!" I dried my face and body, wrapped myself in my robe, and exited the bathroom with pride. The following words out of my mouth were, "You have five days to get out of my house. It. Is. Over!" He looked at me with a look of shock. "Are you serious? I thought you would give me time. I thought you loved me?" My blood began to boil, but I could not respond with anger. It's like God disabled my petty function. "We had a conversation and made an agreement that I would not be disrespected or infected and don't bring home no babies! You did two out of the three; you disrespected me, and she's pregnant!

"Deal off!"

He was my high school boyfriend. He was something that I would never go for, but his pursuit of me triggered my interest. I was raised in a part of town that he could only dream of. He was raised in a neighborhood that I only saw on TV. We were from two different worlds. He was well known in Richmond for being the head of one of the most notorious gangs in the city. Crazy because I had no clue gangs were in Richmond. I was very naïve about some things but well-versed in others. I was selling weed when we met, so I had a little insight into street life. I was still clueless enough to fear the things he was a part of.

The Dogg Pound was the name of a treacherous gang, and I was dating "Ratboy." I wasn't privy to many of the things they were involved in, but I heard many stories. Stories like them showing up at Skateland, 30 deep, only to have a shootout with rival neighborhoods. Or they were doing the same at a local park just to start (and finish) some beef. I really didn't feed into it, though. I never saw that side of him. When I came around, it was all about me. I wasn't allowed to hang on the block. I wasn't allowed to go to a lot of places for fear of retaliation. I felt protected. I felt loved.

I saw past the danger. When I looked into his eyes, I saw that he introduced himself as Jonathan. I saw his desire to protect me mixed with his desire to leave the streets. He tried so hard to impress me with his money, but it didn't work. I had my own, and plus, I'm spoiled. I already had more than what he could offer materially, and that was not the way to my heart. After weeks of begging me to go on a date, I finally gave in. He dressed in his finest b-boy gear (a fresh white tee and some jean shorts); I picked him up, and we went straight to the park.

"Why are we here?" He asked.

"This is our date!"

He was so confused. It was too cute. He clearly had no understanding of how to be with someone without spending money. He was awkward at first. The more we walked, the more comfortable he became with just talking. We learned about all the plants we walked through. We sat in the Japanese flower garden and talked about things far beyond his understanding. At one point, I could see him gazing at the beauty he didn't know existed. The crazy part is we were five blocks away from his stomping grounds.

Time went on, and the fog of puppy love put us in a chokehold. Our conversations were less about the streets and more about the future. We would laugh and play like two kids on the playground. We were just happy to be each other's peace. But I had thoughts about sex. "Why haven't you tried to have sex with me?" I asked, "Is something wrong?" He looked at me with the most confused expression and responded, "I just wanted to take my time with you. I didn't think you wanted to have sex yet." I turned toward him, and we laughed. The laughter faded into a stare. The stare led to a kiss. The kiss led to ecstasy.

He was my first. I got pregnant the first time we had sex. I was 16 and terrified. He assured me that we would be fine even though my gut told me otherwise. My parents didn't approve of him, and neither did the police and people from other neighborhoods. The lifestyle he was living was fast and dangerous. No room for a child or anyone you truly love. How could I bring a child into this dangerous life? The worry only lasted for a moment. Long story short, I believe God looks out for babies and fools, and we were not babies! While using the restroom one day, I experienced excruciating pain and began to pass a lot of blood. We learned in the emergency room that I had miscarried.

After the loss of our child, things went downhill very fast. Things in the street were starting to get out of control, and

Jonathan was in the middle of it all. It got so bad our times together were few and far between. We had our daily talks to hear each other's voices. We had pager codes to communicate when there was no time to pick up the phone. If I didn't get a page or a call at our normal times, I was on the phone calling every hospital and jail until I found him. Thankfully, he called and ensured that he was okay. But one day, things didn't play out that way.

I talked with him early that morning and told him about the events of my day, and we agreed to meet each other around noon. But as the day went on, things just didn't feel right. The normal page I'd get confirming our meeting never came. I went to the spot we agreed to meet and received a message that rocked my world. My love and others were taken away in handcuffs by Richmond's finest. This is where the nightmare began.

Twenty-four years in the Virginia Department of Corrections was his sentence at 17 years old. He tried to keep me away from the chaos until everything was said and done, but my curiosity led me down the rabbit hole. I was floored when I read the charges. I had no idea what crimes he had committed. But oddly, I didn't feel betrayed. I felt protected from the dangers of the streets, and I decided to hold him down. I couldn't turn my back on my love. I didn't see the person they saw. I saw what he could be and wanted to help him get there. I was determined to be there for the entire ride.

I visited every weekend. I spent time and money making sure he had what he needed inside. I was sure to offer encouragement when things got tough. I even went as far as collecting money from those who owed him money. I took pride in holding him down. He protected me, and I needed to return the favor and make sure he was good. I just couldn't entertain the thought of leaving him high and dry while continuing to live my life. I gave it my all.

All of this sounded good at the time, but it began to weigh heavy on me. The adrenaline of being a loyal girlfriend wore off quickly, and I was crumbling. Things got tough around year six. I was in the free world, living life by its terms, and he was locked away with minimal support. The trips up and down the highway became more expensive, and life's demands became my priority. I was becoming a woman in this world while he was stuck at the same age he was when he entered the system.

He became manipulative and very selfish. He was being groomed to be the convict that he needed to be to survive the journey. He got into more and more trouble, which increased his security level. This led to him being transferred to one of the most dangerous prisons in Virginia. After years of allegiance to him in prison, I ended it. I stopped accepting phone calls. I stopped writing letters. I stopped visiting. I gave up on it all.

We spent seven years apart. I got involved in another relationship and had three kids. In my mind, Jonathan was a thing of the past. I was confident that I would never see or hear from him again. But I was wrong. Jonathan found a way to reach out to me through a mutual friend. When I got the call and heard his voice, I froze. "Please don't hang up! I just wanted to say hello." Tears flowed. This felt different. This was the person I fell in love with, not the person I left seven years ago.

His maturity led me to feel like I could love and trust again. I began to visit and write again. Time passed, and things went well between us. We talked every day. He had become my emotional support. He was everything I needed at the time. He knew exactly what to do and say to make me fall deeper in love. One day, in a packed visitation room, Jonathan asked me to marry him, and I said, "Yes!"

We got married on September 3, 2015. Our growing love inspired me to share my love with others who were walking the same path. After years of advocating for my husband and others, I founded a nonprofit organization to provide support to those like me. My husband played a big role in the organization. He never forgot to tell me how proud he was of the work I was doing and took pride in hearing how much help I was to his friends and family.

We were about two years away from his release date, and the convict I had left behind began to show himself. I ignored it and charged it to his nerves, but as time got closer to his release, Jonathan got worse. I continued to ignore him until I couldn't anymore.

A Piece Of Change

On December 21, 2020, Jonathan came home from prison. In a very short time, he showed his true self. The more time we spent together, the things I used to be able to ignore pissed me off more and more. Jonathan was still the same 17-year-old he was when he was incarcerated. He was just in the body of a 44-year-old. Jonathan befriended a female who had every intention of doing what she did: destroy his life. Stories were coming back to me from people in the streets. His behavior was questionable. He had gotten in way too deep, too fast. My heart was broken.

Our marriage was over, and Jonathan had to go. It was a harsh reality for me to accept. When he left the house, he left a note behind with the key attached. The words on the paper set my soul on fire. This man apologized for how things turned out and still expressed how much he loved me. I wanted to go crazy, but all I could do was cry. It was like he didn't even understand how hurt I was.

The next day, I read the letter again. This time, God showed me its true purpose. That letter was confirmation that I made the right move. It showed me that my time with Jonathan was done. There was nothing more I could give him. The union wasn't for love; it was for a lesson. I learned that people are here for a reason or a season, and this season was over. Jonathan needed me to get through a time in his life when he needed support. And though love played a role, it truly had nothing to do with how things turned out. It wasn't love; it was life.

This story could have taken so many turns. Lord knows I have played out every scenario in my head. But I would cause a delay in my healing if I didn't admit that I have played a significant part in our story. Yes, I am a woman who loves hard. Yes, I am the woman that will hold someone down in the worst of times. Yes, I still have a heart for those who need me in the same capacity as Jonathan once did. But now, I know how to be true to who you see without compromising who I am.

So my sister, who is stuck in a place of uncertainty, make the move. God will provide. I know it's scary and somewhat embarrassing to watch something you have built crumble into ashes. But don't burn with it. My anger wouldn't allow me to begin healing. I was so focused on revenge I couldn't see past red. When I finally broke, it hurt so bad. But I continued the work, and because I did, my test is now my testimony. Yours will be, too.

I know it's scary and somewhat embarrassing to watch something you have built crumble into ashes. But don't burn with it.

— **Sonya the SheE.O**

Healing Hatred

Angela N. Jackson

As I searched the internet, I came up short. I couldn't find a single word to adequately capture my feelings as a young child. There were many days I felt happy, protected, loved, and self-assured, but there were also days I found it difficult to smile and hold my head up because I was afraid the people who expected me to be okay would see how hurt I was. I wanted everyone to believe I was okay, but the truth was I felt betrayed, I was angry, and my heart was broken. There was a void, and I didn't know how to fill it. For many years, this emptiness would make me feel as if I had been robbed of a normal childhood.

As a young child, it was fun for me to follow my mom around the house. I just wanted to be close to her, no matter what she did. I specifically remember being in the kitchen when she was washing dishes and listening to music. This song by Shep & The Limelites caught my attention - "Daddy's Home" (1961) is a classic. Of course, I didn't know who they were then, but the lyrics will forever be stuck in my head. "You're the girl of my dreams ...Daddy's home, your daddy's home to stay." As I listened to the words, a sadness embodied me, one that unbeknownst to me would dwell within me for many years. Back then, the artist was very clever in putting lyrics together; whether I grasped the true meaning or not, as a little girl, the words hit me hard. It was at that moment I realized that my daddy wasn't home. I wondered, why not?

Despite being a single mother of four, my mother did her best to raise us. I can still see her wearing that weird-shaped hat on her head while dressed in her nursing uniform. She would be in the mirror checking her hair and putting on makeup. She was so pretty. I would watch her stare into the mirror at herself, and several times, I noticed the wet tears trickling down her cheeks. I wondered how she could cry without making a sound. I, too, would learn to master the skill of a silent cryer one day. Mom was an emergency room nurse, so she was always exhausted when she came home. She would collapse on the couch, and my sisters and I would take turns massaging her feet. Occasionally, she would bring us a treat and give us the PG-rated version of her work night. After a hard workweek, she would somehow muster the energy to wake up early every Sunday morning to get us for church. I enjoyed listening to the preacher because it made me happy to learn about God. However, there were moments when I would wonder why God would allow this unhappiness in my life if He loved everyone and wanted everyone to be happy. Why did He allow my father to leave me?

My father wasn't around. He never dropped me off or picked me up from school. He didn't support me in any school activities or events. He wasn't there for birthdays or holidays.

I was curious about my father's absence, but I wasn't sure how to ask questions. All I knew was that he wasn't with me, and the longing for my father to be around more became a constant poignant feeling. When I reflect on my childhood, there is one recurring memory that comes to me. I was at my cousin's house one day and we were walking around the neighborhood. We passed a house that we had passed many times before but this day as we walked by, my cousin suddenly stopped talking, pointed in the direction of the house, and said "Look Angie, that's your daddy." Before I knew it, my feet were moving more rapidly than a sprinting track star. I don't know what made me run, but I did, and I didn't stop until I was back at my cousin's house. I remember feeling embarrassed because I had not seen my father in so long that I had no idea what he looked like. I guess he recognized me because later that day, the "same man"—my father—came to my cousin's house with gifts. Maybe he felt a sense of embarrassment himself. After all, he should have felt ashamed that his daughter was running away from him instead of into his arms, which is where I really wanted to be. He talked to me and my sister for a few minutes, he hugged us and promised to see us again soon. Months passed and he never showed up.

I was ten when my father began visiting me and my sister regularly. There was always a lot of tension between my parents. When my father came to pick us up, my mother quickly left the room. I guess she did this to avoid

A Piece Of Change

confrontation. He would take us to get candy or ice cream during our visits. I would laugh and pretend that everything was perfect for as long as possible because I knew our time would end, and I would be back home without him. The visits stopped without any notice. Months went by without him calling or coming to pick us up. He would make promises to visit, and we would believe him. We would wait by the window for hours, jumping up to every car we heard pull up, only to see that it wasn't him. There were moments when my older sister would cry, and I would try to comfort her. I convinced myself that he had to have had a major emergency for him to not show up. What could possibly make him not want to see us? What could be stopping him from wanting to spend time with us? We were his little girls. I couldn't understand what was happening, and my mom never talked about it. My mother never said anything about my father's behavior, and it confused me even more. I never understood her reaction to my father's behavior. She didn't seem to fight for his presence in our lives. Nor did she take any steps to hold him financially responsible for his children. Her response taught me to accept a person's worst qualities and not talk about or demand change. My father's actions taught me never to trust or depend on anyone. As a result of observing these harmful behaviors in both, I would later develop unhealthy relationships with other people.

My family did not understand the extent of my pain that was slowly merging into hatred, they just knew that I was upset with my father. I still remember the times I would cry to sleep, imagining what it would have been like to have a dad. By the time I was a teenager, I had never celebrated Christmas, Easter, or my birthday with my father. In addition to my typical teenage emotions, I had to acclimate to yet another significant life adjustment. My sister and I were aware that our father was dating. Still, we were devastated to find out that he was seeing someone with kids and that he would eventually begin living with them. This change was extremely difficult because I had somehow convinced myself he didn't want to spend time with us. He was too busy working, or maybe he didn't want to be bothered with kids, especially girls. Once again, I struggled to understand why he did not choose us. His behavior caused me to constantly wonder if there was something wrong with me. I hated visiting him at his new home because it was a hurtful reminder that those kids were getting something me and my sister weren't, something I always wanted. A father's love.

Eventually, I would begin to blame myself, wondering why I could not let go and accept my father as he was. Years passed and I was now a mother of three. Making sure my children felt loved was always the most important thing to me. I wondered why my father didn't feel the same for me and my sister. I made several attempts to communicate with my father throughout the years. I tried more than once to let him know how I was feeling. I tried to get him to understand how much he disappointed me. I wanted him to say he was sorry. But he never did. I had gotten to the point that I was sick of him, and in my mind, I never had to speak to him again. Out of sight, out of mind was the way I thought. This anguish would cause me to hold on to unforgiveness for a long time. I knew I had to eventually forgive my father because God required me to do so. Many people tried to convince me that I should pardon him, and I knew they were right, but I wouldn't let anyone tell me *when* to do it. I adamantly refused to submit to anyone else's timetable for my healing process. My father was going to have to give me an explanation before I could forgive him. I believed it was the least he could do for me. I was not just going to move on and let go that fast without knowing the reason for his abandonment, neglect, and rejection. I needed to hear why he chose to love and raise someone else children above his own. That was a question I felt deserved an answer. This was *my* pain, that I felt forced to endure. And in my mind, the one thing I could control was deciding when he was worthy of my forgiveness.

When my kids were young, I would help them pick out the perfect Father's Day card for their daddy. I hated reading the Hallmark cards of the perfect fathers. It seemed everyone had a father but me. My children were so excited about what they wanted to buy their daddy. I would watch as they carefully choose the perfect gift or card. The feeling was bittersweet because their relationship with their daddy was special; it was what I wanted with my father. I had hoped that once my kids were old enough to choose their own cards, the hurt would subside, yet every year, I would catch myself thinking back on my hurtful childhood. I went to therapy to understand how to get over the continuous thought pattern that spewed hate. What I learned was that my father's actions shaped me into a woman who hated the idea of needing anything from anyone. I was taught early in childhood that to expect anything from someone is to expose yourself to disappointments, and I detested the feeling of being let down. Before confiding my needs to anyone, I would prefer to suffer in silence - I became a silent cryer just like my mom. Allowing someone to let me down made me feel weak. I learned early to always depend on me, it was my coping mechanism. Silently imploding with anger and hatred kept me broken. And although being broken was draining. I was still not ready to forgive. I knew my heart needed more time to heal this wound.

Then it hit me one day. 2018 Father's Day had just passed, and for whatever reason, that year was extremely hard for me. I have experienced the same feelings for over 30 years and accepted it as a normal pattern of emotions, so why was I crying like this? It was as if I was eight, seventeen, or twenty-five all over again. In the past, feeling that my hatred and deep-rooted anger were justifiable, allowed me to be content in my unforgiveness. But that year felt different; I was tired of despising him. It was time to let it go. It had been too long, and I told myself to refuse to hurt anymore. So, I called him to have the conversation I had attempted many times before. Still, this time, I started the conversation with, "I just need you to listen." I knew it would become another heated conversation if he tried to defend himself. I told my father how I felt. I poured my heart out to him. I told him how much he disappointed me; I told him about the sad five-year-old girl, the abandoned teenager, the hurt woman that I had become. I told him I had tried for years to move past the pain and couldn't. I told him I was exhausted from being emotionally broken and mentally drained from hating him. And on that day, I chose to forgive him. He listened. Surprisingly, he didn't say a word, and when I hung up, I cried. This time, my cry was different - it was full of forgiveness. I felt like he finally got it. He didn't interrupt me; he didn't try to defend himself. He just listened, and, at that moment, I released the anguish from unforgiveness. I felt free and liberated; it was like having a weight taken off my heart. I no longer needed an apology or an explanation from him. I could love him freely once again. I was overjoyed that I had the capacity for forgiveness. It took a long time for me to get to this place., but I'm here. My father and I have made changes in our relationship. We have more conversations, we laugh more, and I visit him more often. It's not perfect, but it's still a work in progress. I no longer view him with the animosity I once had against him.

Through this chapter, I have shared with you the journey of a difficult time in my life during which I was consumed with an immense amount of hurt and anger. I've had countless conversations, shed a lot of tears, and tried my hardest to explain the emotional hurt I experienced. But perhaps the most prevalent piece of change is not whether I can articulate my feelings enough for everyone to understand. It is the individual discovery that painful experiences mold our personalities and are essential for growing as people. Pain is inevitable, but pain also requires boundaries. I had to give my pain a deadline to move forward. I needed to let it go. Hurtful experiences strengthen us and help us to see where we need to make changes. My change in 2018 was forgiveness and acceptance. I had to forgive my father for not being what I needed him to be and accept that I may never receive an explanation or apology from him. While I regret the many years, we lost I am also incredibly appreciative that we had the opportunity to start a new chapter in our relationship. When I look at him, I can see the love in his eyes, feel it in his hug, and hear it in the way he speaks to me.

My love for my father is being *healed*.

Pain is inevitable, but pain also requires boundaries.

— **Angela N. Jackson**

The Heart Shift

Mendy Huff

A flood of emotions overtook me as I lay in bed staring at the ceiling. This day was different- this moment was different. It was my 50th birthday, and sure, I had many birthdays, 49 of them to be exact. We were amid a global pandemic; I had friends and family who had succumbed to the dreadful disease of COVID-19. The world came to a halt, time was lost, and plans were changed. The plan was to celebrate my birthday on a European trip to London, Greece, Paris, and Italy. Instead, I celebrated via Zoom with 50 of my family and friends due to the nationwide shutdown and mandatory quarantine. It wasn't exactly how I envisioned celebrating, but I was grateful just to be alive. That day was when the shift happened, which I call The Heart Shift. It's where I began to reflect and evaluate the matters of my heart. The people and things that bring me joy and laughter, the people and things that brought me pain and heartbreak, and the people and things that brought me sadness. I'm not entirely sure if it was the isolation of the pandemic that spurred this on or just the fact that I was getting older. Still, whatever it was, it made me pause and reflect on my life's journey.

I grew up on the streets of Newark, NJ, once known as the Murder Capital of the United States, surrounded by poverty, drugs, and gangs. This was before cell phones, computers, and cable TV. When kids would rather be outside playing Double Dutch or Hopscotch than be indoors in front of a box fan blowing out hot air. Family always lived close by. My aunts and their children stayed with us from time to time. My uncles would rotate in and out. Cousins were more like sisters and brothers and usually lived next door or down the street. My grandmother lived just a couple of blocks away. Her house was the gathering spot for most family get-togethers. During that time, families tended to live in a cluster, typically within walking distance of each other. Family gatherings were always exciting. Whether we were celebrating a birthday, a barbeque, or a picnic in the park, we were guaranteed to have some good food, fun, and laughter, hear some cussing, and maybe see a fight or two break out. One thing was for certain: family was always there if I was hungry or needed a place to stay for a day or two or maybe longer. There was always a hot plate of food for us to eat and a place to lay our heads.

My mom was the provider, nurturer, and the disciplinarian for my brother and I. She had me at 16, and my brother came seven years later, so most of my life, it was the three of us. My dad was pretty much what I would call a rolling stone, coming and going as he pleased. Mom always made sure our family was provided for. Sometimes, she would work two to three jobs just to make ends meet, and like clockwork, my dad would show up on payday with his hand out for money or his backhand if she resisted. She knew how to stretch a dollar or, as she would say, make a dollar out of 15 cents. My mom taught me survival skills like always being aware of my surroundings, listening to what is being said and not said, and understanding the difference between fight and flight. She was never afraid to throw hands with a stranger, a neighbor, or even a family member, but when it came to my dad, submission was her choice.

My mom and dad had been together since she was 12, so I don't know if it was fear of being alone or a lack of self-esteem. Still, nevertheless, she stayed with him through it all until his dying breath. As a child, I was a daddy's girl. We would sit all day and listen to music from the '70s R&B groups like The Stylistics, Blue Magic, and The Whispers. I was pretty much his shadow. If you saw him, you saw me. Although I loved my dad, I couldn't understand why he would hurt my mom and make her cry. When I was four or five years old, he beat her. I heard her plead with him to stop. So many times, I would go to her and say, "Mommy, don't cry." And she would say, "I'm okay, baby." just the thought of it brings back a burden of sadness and helplessness. As I got older, my relationship with my dad was strained. I could no longer look at him with the same daddy's girl eyes. I could only see him through the eyes of disdain. It was as if a movie clip played on repeat the abuse my mom endured, and the many times he was absent when we needed him most. For example, there have been countless times when the electric company came to cut off our power due to nonpayment or times, they came to cut off the running water. He would be absent in our greatest times of need. How could he do that to us, his family? Why would he spend time with the other woman and her family when his family needed him? These were the questions that were never answered, and to be honest, I never asked, but they continued to fester within me and caused me to divest and disown him. For years, I didn't acknowledge him as my dad. I would make up a story that someone else was my dad and begin to rationalize why he couldn't be my dad, like, "I don't look anything like him" or "I'm taller than both my mom and dad." This was my way of protecting myself, but I still wanted him to hurt like he hurt my mom and me. Finally, I got the chance to do just that on my wedding day. The opportunity came for me to give him a taste of his own medicine. I refused to allow him to walk me down the aisle. Most fathers take the greatest pride in walking their daughters down the aisle on their wedding day, and I took that moment of pride away from him. I didn't want to pretend anymore that his actions, or lack thereof, were acceptable. He cried like a baby because his baby girl, who was once his shadow, was now a grown woman who refused to have him take part in her special day. I was angry and didn't care how anyone felt about it. Everyone, including my mom and soon-to-be husband, tried to convince me to change my mind, but I refused. I stood on all ten toes; this was my day, and he wouldn't be a part of it.

I understand anger was the symptom; unforgiveness was the root. Hurt people hurt people, and forgiveness is the only way to truly overcome the hurt. You don't have to wait for an apology or reconciliation to forgive. True forgiveness is a matter of the heart. It doesn't mean you forget the wrongs or are no longer reminded of the situation. It just means it no longer has power over you.

My breakthrough came as I did my oldest daughter's hair when an overwhelming feeling of love engulfed me. I hugged her and said, "Mommy loves you so much." At that moment, I felt the presence of God. *You understand the depth of love you have for your child. Imagine how much I love you! I forgave you and surely you can forgive him.* I fell on my knees, asked for God's forgiveness, and forgave my dad. I never told him about my encounter with God or asked him why he did the things he did. Nor did I share the negative emotions he caused. I just traded it all for peace and put it at the altar of God. I went from seeing him through the eyes of disdain to seeing him through the eyes of compassion, only by the grace of God. Although the memories were present, the work of forgiveness had begun. One conversation led to another, and then one visit turned into many. When my dad took his last breath, our relationship was good.

There was still work to be done within me.

Unforgiveness can spread to other relationships and can show up in many forms. In my life, it showed up in my marriage. I married my high school sweetheart at the age of 18. We were both young and in love and ready to spend the rest of our lives together. I always had an unwavering trust in my husband's fidelity to our marriage even though we spent many days, weeks, and months apart due to his Naval Career. However, early on, I erected a defensive wall because there were parts of me, I wasn't ready to share with anyone, including my husband. The wounds were too deep, and the healing hadn't truly begun. I became a pro at suppressing my thoughts and emotions, burying them so deep as if the experiences never happened. If I was hurt, I didn't want to talk about it. If I was overwhelmed, I didn't want to talk about it; if I was frustrated, I didn't want to talk about it. I just didn't want to talk about it. Not talking became the problem. A lack of communication and avoiding conflict is some of the biggest reasons marriages end in divorce. Your marriage should be your safe space to share your inner thoughts, beliefs, and desires. For some, it may happen organically. For me, it took years.

When we build an emotional wall, it's a way of protecting ourselves from the hurt and the pain from previous relationships, whether it's family, romantic, or friendships. We tell ourselves, "If I don't allow them in, they can't hurt me." However, we do not realize we're hurting ourselves in the long run. When you block people from getting in, you also block yourself from being free. It becomes a prison, depriving you of the much-needed nutrients to help you grow and thrive, like love, honesty, and mutual respect. Love requires you to break down the wall. To be vulnerable physically, mentally, and emotionally is the price we pay for it.

With over 35 years of marriage, we are entering into a new season that requires some real candid conversations, an investment of time together without the kids, and looking at one another from a different lens. We are no longer the 18- and 20-year-olds trying to figure out married life and parenting. We are now aging, and our needs and assurances must be clearly defined. Can I count on you to be there if something should happen to me, and I can't take care of myself physically? Can you handle wiping my drool or my butt? If I forget, will you help me remember? These are real, mutual, straight-talk questions that need to be answered. Communication is key in any healthy marriage, and understanding of each other's needs, wants, and desires can only be addressed via conversations.

Ultimately, healthy, balanced relationships enrich our lives for the better. When you have a genuine love for one another, it provides a stable source of support, joy, and companionship. We are not meant to be alone. Relationships matter. They serve as a foundation for personal growth and emotional well-being. By ensuring that both parties are equally invested in the relationship, we create a space where both can thrive. Investing time and effort into maintaining healthy relationships is essential for nurturing long-lasting and meaningful connections that stand the test of all seasons.

You don't have to wait for an apology or reconciliation to forgive. True forgiveness is a matter of the heart

— **Mendy Huff**

The Transforming Impact of Love, Faith, and Forgiveness

Rev. Dr. Angela B. Jones

~~~

"With all humility and gentleness, with patience, bearing with one another in love."

— (Ephesians 4:2).

Falling in love

Perry and I fell in love at a young age. It began when I would bring love letters to him from my girlfriends. On Sunday evenings, my grandmother and I would visit my stepgrandfather's family in another town. His nieces and I would talk about everything, especially boys. They would write love letters, spray perfume on the envelopes, and give them to me to deliver to Perry and his brothers. The exchange of letters led Perry and I to be attracted to each other.

At sixteen, I asked my dad if Perry could come visit me at my grandmother's house. My father agreed, and we began to date.

Some evenings, we would go for walks through the town. We never missed a chance to stop at the post office and kiss and fondle each other. Dating offered the opportunity for us to be intimate. We discovered every part of each other's body. I would allow Perry to touch me from head to toe, gently unbuttoning my blouse and caressing my breast, kissing and more kissing. Our intimate desire for one another overcame us so much that we would sneak into an unlocked parked car, drive on dark, deserted roads and school buses during games, anywhere and anytime that we could get together, we did. He was my first love, and I have trusted him with my whole life.

A few months after dating, things seriously changed. I missed my period. My mother made me a doctor's appointment. I was frightened and began to pray that I wasn't pregnant. The pregnancy test came back positive. I rode home, looking out the back windshield with tears in my eyes. When I got home, I ran into my room, buried my face in my pillar, and cried.

The next time I saw Perry, I told him the news. He seemed to be in denial and said something stupid like, "Is it mine?" I responded, "What, who else did you give me time to be with?" He quickly dropped that thought and began to accept responsibility.

I felt devastated and embarrassed. I had disappointed everyone. All through my pregnancy, I was in denial and told my dad that I didn't do anything; I continuously denied even having sex. My grandmother was upset and desperate. She gave me something to drink for anemia. My period came back, and my secret of having sexual intercourse was hidden.

I was relieved. I was never going to be intimate with Perry again. Everything was back to normal, and I could breathe.

However, my period only lasted a day when panic set in. What was I to do? I was being rejected at my church, and my uncle asked me to apologize in front of them. My school would not let me participate in activities. I wanted to run for May Queen and was told I couldn't. I wish I could turn time back. I wanted so badly not to be pregnant. I got on my knees by my bed and asked God to not let me be pregnant. *Whatever I could do, Lord, I was all for it.*

My grandmother saw my disparity and continued to try to rectify the situation. She arranged for me to go to New Jersey to have an abortion. My cousin was pregnant too, so we were to go together. My mother heard about the arrangements and came that evening and picked me up from my grandmother's house and saved my baby's life. A part of me was relieved. What a big mistake my grandmother and I could have made by taking this innocent life. My mother saved my baby.

My body began to change. As the months went by, I vomited and felt nauseated throughout the day. My grandmother explained that it was morning sickness. The baby was moving, kicking, and growing. My grandmother did domestic work, mainly in the non-black neighborhoods, and she would gather the old, discarded dresses of the homeowner and make my maternity dresses. Two of the dresses were so special to me. She made me this flowered golden dress with large pleats gathered around the top of my pregnant stomach, hanging loosely down below my knees to wear to church. Both of us had a change of heart from desperation and disappointment to acceptance and forgiveness.

Next, she made me a prom dress to go to Perry's senior prom. She made me a beautiful long white dress with a silk satin slip underneath the lacy skirt, hanging straps, and long lacy sleeves. I pretended that it was a wedding dress. The girls were envious of my dress and my date, my prince charming, my baby's daddy escorting me, treating me like a queen. He brought me straight home after the prom.

Two months later, it was time for the baby to be born. My water broke, and there was a lot of pressure and pain in my stomach. In the hospital, there was unbearable discomfort. The baby was a breeched birth, resulting in a brachial plexus injury. Our baby girl, Portia, was beautiful. Being parents sealed our love forever.

Faithful transformation

"But without faith, it is impossible to please God" (Hebrews 11:6).

Faith Endures

Perry and I believed that we would be together soon. After graduating from high school, he joined the military and enlisted in the 82nd Airborne Division at Fort Bragg, N.C.

We were miserable being apart. I wouldn't graduate until two years later. My grandmother suggested that I go to college. I hesitated, but I went for one year and received a cosmology diploma. On the day of my graduation, Perry went AWOL (absent without official leave) to get married, eventually growing our family. Our baby girl, Angenette, was born at Fort Bragg, N.C. Our first son, Perry Jr., was born in Hanau, Germany. Roderick was born at Langley Airforce base, Hampton, Va. Our youngest son, Ronalvon, was born in Newport, Va. By faith, our dream came true. We were a big, happy family.

In 1990, we were able to buy a house for our large family. Soon afterward, Perry received orders to go to Panama. We discussed whether we should go as a family. In our 17-year marriage, we had never been separated any longer than two weeks when he was training in the fields. But we had just bought the house. What would we do with it? Perry decided to go alone and take a two-year instead of a three-year tour. Faithfully, we would endure this separation.

About one month after Perry went to Panama, he changed. The letters, phone calls, and money stopped. I became so concerned, thinking about his well-being. I would gather quarters and put ten dollars' worth in the phone booth just to hear his voice for three minutes. I loved him so much. It was so unlike him not to communicate.

I decided to convert my garage into a beauty shop. I had a good clientele. It was very difficult to focus on my work. I developed anxiety and depression, and all I talked about was how I wasn't hearing from Perry. One day one of my customers turned the styling chair around, looked me in the face, and said, "Angela, there's another woman. Your husband is cheating on you." My customer shocked me by saying that. Another woman had never entered my mind. "What? No, there's no other woman. No, No, No, you're wrong. He wouldn't do that; he loves me and only me." I broke down and cried uncontrollably. I had been in denial. What else could have happened? He was sleeping with another woman. I put my face in my hands, crying: He was my love, my husband, my children's father. I gave up my dreams in life so we could be together. This could not be true!

I had to face reality. A devastating change had come over our marriage. My husband was sleeping with another woman. The next time I called, the woman answered the phone. I was furious and asked him who she was. He said, "The maid." I knew all the time that he was lying. He no longer supported us, the money was gone, we lost our home, but I didn't lose my children. By faith, help from our church, and the older children working, we survived the dramatic change.

By accident, I learned that Perry had another child. My baby got sick, and I had to take him to the military base hospital. As the registrar was registering us, she asked, "Which child is this?" She began to read off names. I said, "That last name is not one of my children. That is a mistake. You need to remove that name." She said, "It's not a mistake. Your husband had this name added recently." I held myself together, fought back the tears, and focused on my baby lying in my arms, sick. I don't wish this kind of pain on anyone, loneliness, abandonment, helplessness, betrayal, deception, and lying. There were times when I felt like giving up, just to be relieved of the negative thoughts of seeing them together intimately. The constant voices I heard in my head caused so much pressure that one day, I fainted. I reached for the phone and called 911. The operator questioned me over the phone and felt as though my symptoms were only an anxiety attack, and she recommended that I go to my doctor, who gave me an appointment to see a therapist. Talking to someone made a difference to my mental health. In one of our sessions, she asked me a profound question, "Where is your faith?"

My faith? I felt too weak to believe in anything. This heartache was for real; I felt suffocated. I was no longer happy. It felt like someone close to me had died, my marriage. I had to go and see for myself. The generosity of my customers helped me to earn enough money to go to Panama.

I bought my ticket and packed for Panama. I believe one of my sisters came and stayed with my children. When I arrived, another family was staying with him. I could not tell what was going on; so many people were in and out of the civilian housing that he was staying in; a woman was there, and there were three small children. In Perry's room, there were no family pictures. The room was very cold and dense. He pretended with me. He had changed from my husband to a stranger. He stressed that I should go back home and take care of the children. He promised that he would be home soon. Part of me wanted to believe him.

"Be kind to one another, kindhearted, forgiving one another, as God in Christ forgave you" (Ephesians 4:32).

Forgiveness Heals

Forgiveness heals a broken spirit. Yes, I was broken into pieces. Love and faith in my marriage caused me to hold on to my husband. Before I left Virginia for Panama, I packed a prayer cloth and placed it under Perry's mattress the day I left. Suddenly, I was no longer burdened with fear and anxiety. I placed the situation in God's hands. I had done what I needed to do, and that was to leave a symbol of faith.

I returned home and embraced my children, feeling relieved and excited about moving forward. They needed me, and I needed them. My son Roderick seemed to have needed me the most. Many nights, I would find him sitting at the foot of my bed, worried about me. I would pull him close to me. He said, "Mom, either way, it's going to be all right." My children saved my life.

Two years went by, my husband returned home and acted as if nothing had ever happened. He was stationed in

Maryland and would stay up there during the week and come to Virginia on the weekends. He had my car. Eventually, signs of a woman and children showed up in the car. They came back with him. I confronted him; He never told the truth, just lied. I was so angry I jumped on his back and started choking him. I came to myself and let him go. He left and didn't come around anymore. One of my customers insisted on driving me to Maryland to get my car. I had an extra set of keys, and we drove off in my car as he came out of the building startled and shouting. I felt a sense of satisfaction for upsetting his day. Two years later, he retired and moved to Virginia. I heard they were near. One night, I left my children and tried to find them. That night was so dark and dreary that I got lost. I was confused and frightened. I pulled over to the side of the road and prayed. I said, "Father, if you get me home, I promise not to look for them again." Prayer shifted my thoughts. A change came over me. My children needed me. God took the steering wheel and guided me home. I can not imagine what possibly could have happened if I had found them? God stepped in on time and changed me.

During the fifteen years of separation, I went back to school and received a BA, MA, and MDIV degrees. Three of my children were grown, and I moved to Richmond, VA, with the two younger boys. I taught in public school, attended seminary, received my ministerial license, became the youth leader at my church, and traveled to Canada and Africa. My son Roderick and I bought a house and were living our best lives. Later, my younger sons graduated, and I was in Richmond all alone. Through the years, we never did hear from Perry. My youngest son found out where he lived and wanted to go to a school in the area, and I ended up staying with him. Perry lived alone, and I don't know what happened to the woman and the children, even to this day.

We spoke often discussing concerns of my son. Talking with him no longer seemed like torture. It's because I chose to forgive him and her. I was no longer angry or feeling the pain of abandonment and betrayal. I had a peace within me, God's reward when I forgave.

After communicating and visiting for a couple of years, in 2005, my husband and I reunited as husband and wife. We renewed our 50th-anniversary wedding vows last year. The journey wasn't easy. There are still hidden figures.

Whatever *Piece of Change* that might come in your life to destroy you, redirect your mindset by changing yourself. Stir up the gifts that God has placed inside of you, through Love, Faith, and Forgiveness.

*Whatever **Piece of Change** that might come in your life to destroy you, redirect your mindset by changing yourself.*

— Rev. Dr. Angela B Jones

A Silent Apology

Charmaigne L. Lloyd

Life has a brutal way of tearing even the strongest among us apart. Every time I reflect on it, I can barely distinguish between the petty, heartless bastards you are. I sit here, crying, frustrated, wondering where this rage originated. The harder I try to unravel it, the more it ensnares me, dragging me deeper into a vortex of turmoil and agony. The void left by the love of the two people who should mean everything—a father and a mother—is a wound that festers endlessly. It's all wrong, so painfully, devastatingly wrong. As I sit here emotionally on a see-saw trying to determine who caused the most pain.

Growing up, I can remember the praise my family raised when talking about my daddy. However, every time I think back to the day you left, I can't help but curse you silently— a trifling, inconsiderate bastard. I was just a four-year-old girl, sitting on the porch with my brother George, watching as you packed up our lives into that truck, piece by piece. The thought of my mom was nowhere to be seen. Tears streamed down my brother George's and my face as we struggled to grasp what was happening. I knew you were taking things, but I didn't realize it was the start of a life without my father.

I gazed at my dad's smile and quick movements that masked the betrayal against the mother who'd cared for his children.

Mom's humiliation was tangible as she raced down the block, desperate to see what my dad had done. She dashed into the house only to find it emptied of memories that we had all once shared. I remember her screaming, stating, "Even the drapes." As I watched her collapsing in anger and hurt, it appeared she understood the depth of my dad's betrayal. However, my brother and I were too young to even comprehend what had just taken place right in front of my eyes. My grandfather, Woody, allowed this tragic stripping of my mother's home to take place. Woody sat silent, oblivious and unconcerned about the theft happening right under his nose. The disbelief of losing someone I loved so suddenly was overwhelming. It was not just my dad who had left physically, but the heart of my mother was shattered as well.

Living as an adolescent without my father was an experience that deeply affected my social identity and development. His absence left a void that was hard to fill, and I often felt lost and unsure of myself. I missed out on crucial lessons that only a father could teach, such as navigating relationships, handling conflict, and embracing my worth. Without his guidance and support, I struggled to understand my place in the world and how to build meaningful connections with others. The emotional pain of not having him there was overwhelming; I often wished for his presence during important milestones and everyday moments. This lack of a paternal figure not only shaped my self-esteem but also impacted my ability to form healthy relationships, leaving me grappling with feelings of inadequacy and longing for a bond that was never fully realized.

I felt the profound absence of a nurturing mother who was physically present but emotionally detached. Her battle with alcoholism created a wall between us, making it difficult for me to seek the love and support I desperately needed. Instead of comfort, I often faced verbal and mental abuse, which left deep scars on my self-worth. The chaos of our home was compounded by her choices as various unstable individuals entered our lives, fostering an environment where I learned to depend on men for validation, often in unhealthy ways. This dependency developed out of a desperate need for connection, but it only led to further trauma and pain. I found myself navigating a world that felt unsafe and unloving, struggling to break free from cycles of abuse and searching for a sense of belonging that always seemed just out of reach.

One day, I came home to find my mother holding a letter that had slipped from my backpack, a letter from a friend expressing concern about how I was feeling after losing my virginity. The moment she read those words, everything changed. Instead of offering support or understanding, she unleashed her anger and confusion on me, physically engaging in harmful behavior that left me terrified and broken. All throughout the night, she lashed out aggressively, each thought of what had happened fueling her rage, as I felt more alone and scared than ever. I could not wait for the sun to rise the next day so I could escape her presence. When I went to school, my appearance must have raised alarms; I was called to the nurse's office because my sadness was so apparent, and the visible marks on my skin told a story that words could not. Social services were contacted, and I was removed from my home and placed in emergency foster care, where everything felt foreign and unsettling. The experience left me emotionally shattered, filling me with an overwhelming rage against my mother and an unshakeable fear that haunted me from that day forward. I never imagined that the person who was supposed to love and protect me could become the source of my deepest pain.

But then it happened again, another hit to my heart, my mother decided to abandon us to move in with a man; it shattered my understanding of family and safety. Losing our home was already devastating, but her choice to leave my brother and me with a friend—someone we hardly knew—felt like a betrayal. I remember the confusion and sadness that washed over me as she walked out the door, leaving us behind without a second thought. The sense of instability was overwhelming; we were thrust into an unfamiliar environment, trying to adjust to a life without the comfort of our mother. It felt as if she had chosen her new life over us, and I couldn't help but wonder what we had done to deserve such abandonment.

Eventually, she returned, moving us into a home with this new man who seemed to care little for us and was openly jealous of the relationship we shared with our mother. It was heartbreaking to witness how she could choose someone who didn't care for her children, prioritizing his needs over ours. His resentment created a tense atmosphere, and I felt the warmth of our family bond slowly eroding. The love and protection we once had were replaced by uncertainty and fear, leaving me to grapple with the reality that the person who should have been our greatest ally had chosen a life that left us feeling neglected and unwanted.

The constant avoidance of being around alcoholism and the arguments that filled our home left me feeling trapped and desperate for a way out. My self-esteem had sunk so low that I found myself turning to anyone who would offer me a fleeting sense of satisfaction. This cycle began with sexual encounters with older men, a pattern that repeated itself, driven by a need for rebellion in a way that I couldn't fully comprehend at the time. Each encounter felt like a silent cry for help, a misguided attempt to reclaim some control over my life. And then it happened—I decided to stay out late with my friend's older brother, fully aware that mental and physical abuse would likely follow. But at that moment, I was so overwhelmed by everything that was happening around me that I didn't care about the consequences. I was consumed by my anger and hurt, and the thought that the situation could get worse barely registered in my mind. It was as if I was standing on the edge of a cliff, ready to jump into the unknown, ignoring the reality of the dangers that awaited me below.

Oh my God, I cannot believe this is happening. Dear diary, May 1994. Here I am, pregnant and terrified, and of course, my dad is nowhere to be found. I can't believe my mother is doing this to me—forcing me to get an abortion at six months pregnant. What kind of twisted nightmare is this? The sheer cruelty of this experience is beyond anything I've ever faced; she stripped me of my voice, my heart, my trust, and the only love I thought I knew. The way she treated me during this hellish process was unbelievably harsh; I didn't deserve any of it. She made me endure two agonizing days of labor and dragged me back and forth for over twelve hours for a mistake I made—one that could have been avoided if I'd had someone in my life to actually teach me about the harsh realities of growing up. Sure, I messed up, but that mistake spiraled into a raging rebellion and deep-seated anger. She had no clue what I was going through; she didn't care at all. All of this set me up for a life of failures, hopping from one man to another, trapped in one toxic situation after another. I didn't even know what love truly was. I was desperately searching for a father's love in all those men, thinking that love equated to sex because the only man who ever said he loved me was just a predator luring me into his bed—and that's all he ever wanted.

At 19, I was raped and contracted a sexually transmitted disease that shattered me, pushing me to the brink where I wanted to end it all. By 25, I had already endured six abortions, two miscarriages, and given birth to two children with two different fathers. I had been with so many men, each encounter leaving a mark on my soul. I couldn't wrap my head around how someone could be so cruel, so intentionally harmful. The fear of someone harming my baby girl as she slept in her room was mind-boggling, leaving me feeling utterly powerless. Everything I had done in my past caught up to me like a relentless thorn in my side. I felt trapped in a cycle of disappointments and failures, all stemming from the hurt of a mother and father who failed to care for me. The encounters kept piling up, and my self-esteem and self-worth plunged so low that it felt like they were irretrievable. My pain ran so deep that healing seemed like an impossible journey, and I realized I had to start from scratch, like a child learning to navigate the world again. The exposure to drugs, toxic relationships, and violence turned my life into a dizzying merry-go-round, and I became paralyzed by fear of everything around me. It all stemmed from my father's selfishness, seeking a separate life, and my mother's alcoholism clouded her judgment to the point of blacking out and becoming belligerent. My life suffered profoundly, and I lost sight of who I was. I was crying out for an identity, desperate for something I didn't even know how to define. The wounds cut so deeply that I found myself making the same mistakes repeatedly, seeking validation from others to feel like I meant something, to feel like I was somebody. My confidence was nowhere to be found.

After my first child, I exposed her to homelessness and fleeing across the country on Greyhound running from her intimidating, abusive father, I found myself involved with a man who intimidated me even more greatly. His presence was so overpowering that I felt compelled to engage with him, even when every instinct told me to stay away. Instead of standing up and saying no, I let my fear fester, never imagining that I would commit the ultimate sin: betrayal. I was unknowingly involved in a relationship with a married man, having sex and having a child with someone I never thought I'd be with. I knew I had to escape, so I ran as far away as I could, ending up in Richmond, Virginia. There, I had the chance to give myself to the Lord, but once again, I found myself following someone else's path, doing what others were doing, because I lacked my identity. Yet, in that search, I encountered the love of the Lord, even as I continued to grapple with who I was. The cycles of seeking acceptance persisted, not only with men but in all my relationships and life situations. I was still angry at the woman, my mother, who had caused the deepest wounds in my life. In a moment of desperation, I decided to reach out to her with a letter, expressing how deeply she had hurt me because I wanted to heal. I craved something different, knowing that the wounds were tearing me apart inside. I didn't know how to mend them or how to avoid repeating the same mistakes. I longed to develop a sense of confidence in who I was and who I was. When I finally wrote to her, apologizing for my mistakes and hoping she would apologize, she reacted angrily. She couldn't accept the truth of what she had done, the life she had exposed me to that led to my destruction. Instead of acknowledging my pain, she turned away in denial, refusing to apologize. That only deepened the separation between us, but strangely, I was okay with it. I just wanted to heal, to hear her say, "I'm sorry. I apologize for the abortions, for the violence, for the fear I instilled in you." But she refused, and as time went on without her calling—just as she never did—I found peace in that distance. It allowed me to have a clearer mind and an open heart to embrace what I needed to expose and confront within myself.

It was the invitation to *The Change Experience* event in 2022 that I knew I couldn't miss—a moment that prompted me to reflect on the apology I had been desperately seeking, the sympathy I craved, and the peace I longed for from those around me. I realized I didn't need their validation to become who I am. My transformation experience came when I heard a gentle voice whisper in my ear, asking, "What if you never get that apology? What if they never say

I'm sorry?" In that instant, as tears flowed, I understood that my life was poised for a profound change.

Losing one of the closest people to me forced me to confront a painful truth: it was never meant to be a dependency, and it was time to let go. I began to speak the promises that had been whispered to my heart. I started declaring affirmations into the atmosphere, reminding myself that I was called according to a greater purpose, that I was enough, that I was courageous, and, most importantly, that I was worthy.

It was at that pivotal moment that I found the strength to push through the pain. I realized that life would inevitably bring a multitude of losses, but amidst it all, I vowed never to lose my confidence. This journey has shaped me, and now I stand firm in my truth, ready to embrace the future with open arms.

My pain ran so deep that healing seemed like an impossible journey, and I realized I had to start from scratch, like a child learning to navigate the world again.

— **Charmaigne L Lloyd**

No Longer Voiceless: My Cinderella Story

Natasha Broughton

I just wish I would have never done it. But because I didn't say anything, I've lived a life full of cringe-ful regret.

It was the end of 2017, and I was in a situation I'd never thought I'd be in. I was in a sorority, getting attention, and shit, I was trying to be a hoe. If I'm honest, I was a hoe. I just wanted to live my life, be free, and have fun. I had no real responsibilities, and I just wanted to enjoy my late twenties like everybody else. The problem was I wasn't like everyone else. I couldn't do what I wanted, and deep down, I knew it, but I wanted to do it anyway. I was in the club every weekend, at every happy hour spot, and always in a situationship. I was the girl who a guy could take home at night, and I wouldn't question what we were or if he was really interested. However, deep down, I've always wanted to be swept off my feet by Prince Charming. I wanted to be like Cinderella when she lost her shoe, and the Prince came to find her. I wanted that. I wanted my happy ending, or did I want Cinderella's happy ending? Nevertheless, that never seemed to be my story. For as long as I can remember, I've been searching for love and acceptance in all the wrong places. I wanted to be loved and accepted to the point where I compromised my voice for the safety of others.

Living a life of cringeful regret caused me to continuously shame myself for making a choice that others felt was best for me. Merriam-Webster defines cringe as shrinking in fear or servility. Servility is an excessive willingness to serve or please others. I was constantly listening for everyone else to tell me what Natasha should do and how I should feel. I'd never felt safe enough to express my feelings or vocalize what I needed to do for me. Instead, I just began to pull the tape from the dispenser and place it over my mouth every time someone gave their opinion of what I should do by not speaking up. Later on, I would find that not speaking up cost me my voice, and the suffocation had begun.

I had never been so sick before. For weeks, I could not understand why. I'd thought it was the weather change or my demanding work schedule. I just needed to catch up on rest and take better care of myself, I thought. I could not have imagined what would have happened next. I remember being in the bathroom, getting ready to shower for the night. "Are you pregnant?" the text notification came across the screen. *Pregnant?* I thought. Is he crazy? "Hell no, I'm not pregnant," I responded. "Are you sure? Because I feel like it's a possibility that you could be." *What the fuck do you mean a possibility?* I reassured the person that, no, I was not pregnant, and my cycle was about to come. A few days later, I had a braid client, and I remember doing her hair. I began to feel this needle-like sensation in my stomach, so I went to the bathroom. It was probably just my period on the way. However, when I looked down, I saw spotting. I knew this all too well. I've had plenty of friends who have experienced this same exact thing. A million thoughts raced through my mind. I can't be there's no way; it just can't be so. I was in a relationship but not with the person who was on the other side of those text messages. I remember texting my friend Gilly and asking her what she thought. She reassured me that I was, in fact, experiencing pregnancy symptoms and I needed to go to the store. After my client, I went to Walmart and grabbed three pregnancy tests. Before I took the test, I knew. But I proceeded anyway and took the test. Minutes went past as I paced, texting Gilly and praying to God that this test would somehow be negative. The first test result was positive, the second test was positive, and after the third test, I knew for sure I was in trouble. I texted Gilly and said girl, "I'm packing my bag because my mom gone kick my ass out!" I asked her if I could come stay with her in North Carolina for a few months until I got a job and could get out on my own. She said, "Girl, yes, of course!" I sank to the floor in shame, shock, and a whole bunch of *What the fuck did I do? And how was I supposed to tell my mom, my then-boyfriend, and the baby's daddy?* He already had two kids of his own. Yeah, so here I am, another statistic, another baby mama, and knowing damn well I was in no position to take care of a kid. I went back and forth in that bathroom for hours, questioning how the hell I was supposed to tell my mom that I, the minister's daughter, was pregnant by someone that I was not even with.

I went back and forth looking in the mirror, crying uncontrollably, screaming on the inside, disappointed, questioning my life, wondering how the hell could I end up pregnant by a nigga that doesn't even want you. How could I? What are people going to think about the Minister's daughter being pregnant and single? How would they treat me? Again, how the hell am I going to tell my mom that I'm pregnant? Do I move out without telling her anything about the pregnancy? If I tell her, will she shame me? I knew for sure she would kick me out. I finally gathered the strength a few hours later.

I remember going to Mom's room and sitting on the side of her bed, scared to death, and all I muttered was, "I'm pregnant." I didn't have the strength to look her in her face because I didn't want to see the shame that it caused her. My mother only had two questions, "Whose is it?" and "Can you afford a child?" She'd adamantly stated that she was not taking care of a child. I had mixed emotions about her reaction because she'd always taught me to take care of my responsibility, but here she was, telling me I had a decision to make. I was pissed at her. Are you crazy? Did she not care about what I wanted? Did she not hear what she just asked me to do? An abortion? I never thought that would be an option for me. Natasha, having an abortion? Naw. Not me. I knew I was out there hoeing, but to have an abortion, hell no! I had heard enough stories from my friends, and I knew damn well I was not trying to go down that route. Fuck no, not an option. With all the constant tug of war in my mind and without honoring my feelings, I silently gave in and had an abortion. Yeah, the one thing that would lead me to a life filled with regret.

You're probably wondering, what does an abortion have to do with Cinderella? Cinderella and I were very much twins. She didn't use her voice, and neither did I. Cinderella had countless opportunities to speak up, but she chose to shrink and allow others to dictate her story. Just like Cinderella, I dummied myself down and allowed others to speak up for me. I knew damn well I didn't want an abortion, but I refused to speak up. Speaking up made me feel small, but because I never used my voice, I didn't understand the cost of not using my voice. In the moments when I had enough courage to say something, I felt shitted on, and as a result, I added another layer of covering to ensure I remained silent. Cinderella shouldered the responsibilities of her household when she could have very well stood up for herself. I cringe when I think about Cinderella's story because I, too, carried the weight of what others thought and, in the process, kept my damn mouth shut for fear of being heard.

I spent months after the abortion constantly replaying that day in my head. If I would have stopped trying to be a damn hoe, then I would have never been in the situation in the first place. If I had stopped trying to be like everyone else, then the circumstances would have been different. But that wasn't my reality. The reality was Natasha had some identity issues and needed to acknowledge that she was the problem. It wasn't the alcohol, the club, sex, men, my mom, it was me. I was the problem. I prided myself on being the only one of my friends who did not have a child out of wedlock. This was all a part of my identity crisis.

So, the question became, how in the world do I begin the healing process? I had to come to grips with the fact that I had given my power away, my God-given voice. It was extremely difficult to find my voice after relinquishing it to others for so long. After continuous cycles of being silent, I played around with asking God for help. I didn't fully understand or believe that He could help me. But at this point, there were no other options. God was the one who had formed me and knew me before the abortion and after. I stopped trying to heal in my own strength, and when God gave me a way of escaping to heal properly, I took it. I'd spent many nights crying, questioning, frustrated, and hating myself for the choice that I made. But one night, I said no more. I was tired of wearing Cinderella's ball gown in public but in private, wearing hand-me-downs as I swept my issues and insecurities under the rug. I had to forgive myself and acknowledge that I was His daughter. I was still fearfully and wonderfully made in the image of God. He didn't hate me, and He didn't shun me. He loved me. No mistake was too great for Him to stop caring for me and for Him to leave me broken. I was enough for Him to heal, transform, and set me free. Free from guilt, free from shame, and free from all the layers that had silenced my voice.

Just like I started to heal, you can, too. The truth of the matter is my suffocation was self-inflicted. I blamed others, but it was my hands that put the tape over my mouth. God gives each of us a voice, but it is our responsibility to use it. We are required to speak up, even if it's against our own thoughts. I had to know that my voice had the power to break cycles generational curses, and the ability to help others. Please understand that your healing is possible, but you must want to be healed. Just like the woman with the issue of blood, God asked her if she wanted to be made well. He gave her a choice. So, my question to you is pretty much the same, do you want to be healed? You can take your power back. Pull the tape from your mouth and speak. Don't suffer in silence any longer. Refuse to succumb to the story that left you in pieces. Instead, create your own story and choose healing, forgiveness, and love of self.

Refuse to succumb to the story that left you in pieces. Instead, create your own story and choose healing, forgiveness, and love of self.

— **Natasha Broughton**

A Glimpse of Metamorphosis

Leona Elzy

～

The old verbiage *sticks and stones may break my bones, but words will never hurt me. It* is a Pinocchio's tale if I have ever heard one. There were many times when words spoken to me or about me caused the most painful sensation imaginable, even more painful than a splinter beneath the fingernail ouch.

My family didn't have much money growing up, and my sisters and I usually wore hand-me-downs or thrifted items. If we got anything new, it was from either Walmart or the local bargain store Gators. This left me open to constant ridicule or ribbing, as we refer to it in New Orleans. In the 2018 Marvel movie The Black Panther, there was a phrase I had heard most of my life "What are those?" a phrase jokingly spewed to the main character King T' Challa by his younger sister Shuri as she mocked a pair of sandals he wore. To add insult to injury, I have always been the shy, quiet girl with minimal words, so much so a few people thought I was mute. Because of these irrelevant things, I was an easy target, and those words hurt me. My peers weren't the only ones delivering crude and crass remarks. My mom would callously scorn me for being the grey-eyed heifer that nearly caused her to lose her life due to postpartum hemorrhaging on the delivery table. When boys started to take an interest in me and I in them, almost instantly, I became a hot ass and somehow would give birth to 99 babies, all by the age of fifteen. Starting my period for the first time was terrifying and humiliating; I was forced to lie on my back as my mother and aunt inspected my vagina and openly debated that I was possibly having sex with a man because, logically, a young boy wouldn't have been able to cause me to bleed before they ultimately concluded that I was indeed at the age of menstruation. After wadding me up with old rags, I was sent off to the middle school with no instruction or knowledge of what further to do about it.

Koryn Hawthorne melodically sings the words "Felt so bad I thought I would die' in her 2017 debut Gospel single- Won't He Do It, but in 1996, it was the reality I lived that led to my first attempt at suicide.

Though Jesus said, in Luke 4:4 "People do not live by bread alone."; as my conscious awareness wavered between dreamland and reality, I clearly recall the bits of bread being shoved into my mouth by my eleven-year-old sister as she feebly attempted to save my life, and the words, "Let her die, I have insurance on her," pierced the membranes of my ears and arrested the chambers of my heart. Those words were vehemently spewed from the mouth of my mother. I don't know why that response shocked me, but tears began to form as sleep overcame my body. The pills didn't claim my life that day, but there was a murder by words. How could the one person specifically designed to nurture and care for me be so cruel and filled with discontent towards their own offspring?

Like barricades on a parade route, God had taken favor upon me and blocked my mother's chance to cash in on that insurance policy, so I decided to take that opportunity to live to protect my two younger sisters, Amiga and Shirdesha. Writing poetry became the wonderland in which I would escape, and music was the rabbit hole that would take me there. Most of my poems were written about Carlos, my high school sweetheart. We were the Romeo and Juliet of the hood, living, breathing sonnets with a story to tell. No vials of poison were consumed, but the waves of adolescence kept knocking me down. He, like most teenage boys, started lying and sneaking around with other girls, so I was left drowning in my own tears. I would play and rewind my radio-recorded mixed tape of "The Arms of the One Who Loves You," a hit record from the album Traces of my Lipstick by Xscape. Yes, I know that's illegal, but all the kids were doing it, besides I own the actual CD now, so shh.

WHY?

3/5/1998
I really want to know
How far my love will grow
Sometimes I wonder why,
When I think about your Love

I feel as though I'll cry.
So, I say to you today
I Love you in every way
But the Love you give to me
I simply cannot repay.
Four months later…

Do you Know?

7/14/1998
Do you know what it's like,
To be in Love?
Do you know what it's like,
To be played for a fool?
Do you know what it's like,
To not feel Loved?
Do you know what it's like,
To not have any friends?
Do you know what it's like,
To not have a shoulder to cry on?
Do you know what it's like,
To feel all alone?
And
Do you know,
That I wish I didn't!

A few of the many poems written from my emotional fourteen-year-old heart, I never imagined I'd be sharing it with the world. As you continue to read my chapter remember me as being in the Pupa stage of my life as a butterfly. Until this point, I had been the very hungry caterpillar feeding on the experiences of life that presented as breadcrumbs.

Everything was changing so quickly; I went from being his one to being the one reading a letter he had stuffed inside a drawer from another girl exclaiming how much she missed hanging out and watching Arthur with him. As I stared at her smiling face posing in jean overalls, one strap clipped and the other dangling while hugging a stuffed Tweety bird, the ugly face of reality emerged. I quickly copied her address from the envelope before he came back into the room. Although this girl had moved to Ohio, I had to write to her and let her know about me, too. In her response to me, she wrote she had not been aware of me. She must have also written to him because one afternoon, he called my house upset and screaming at me because I had gone through his things and written to this girl. We had our first break up that day. Hanging up the phone, the thoughts in my head galloped hastily as if in a race with the rhythm of my heart. Each lub dub emitted an agonizing feeling, and I wanted it all to stop. I searched the drawers for the bottle I just knew would be able to take the pain away. In the same way, my eyes would change from green to blue, and so did my mood. The pills I clenched in my fist would surely ease it all. I consumed at least twenty pills at once and chased them with enough water to extinguish a small fire. Yes, it would all be over soon. For about three minutes, I had complete confidence that the afflictions I wrestled with would soon be put to rest for good. A familiar sensation began to build in my stomach, quickly and suddenly escalating into a rolling storm that forcibly burst forth from my lips, expelling the entire contents of my stomach in a torrent of vomit. As my abdomen contracted and my body convulsed with fierce intensity, my body purged itself of the poison with no assistance from me or any medical team. Later in life, I would come to realize that it was the Holy Spirit intercepting one of my foolish plans. Exhausted and confused reality set in that not only had suicide attempt number two failed, but I was going to have to clean up that mess and later explain what had happened to those pills.

"Kiss me back," He moaned over my clenched lips as I sat with my eyes closed and wished this wasn't happening to me. How could he? Why would he? His hands were on my breast as he slid closer to the couch, and then I heard the lock on the door rattle. Someone was trying to get in, so I would be safe. My stepsister was right on time to ward off the molestation in progress; I made sure never to be alone with my dad again. Once, being a Daddy's girl, the question was asked, why don't you talk to your dad anymore? I would avoid that question for almost six years.

Fast-tracked on the wheel of life, I was determined to get out. Out of the house, the city, hell, maybe even the state. I needed to be as far away as possible from the mockery of my peers and family. Within my first year of being in the Navy, I fell head over heels into another incredible love story that, like the last one, I was sure would never end. Ironically, that story ended halfway through my next set of orders, and it, too, was a quarter past time for lies and cheating. Myron, my fiancé who was still in Illinois while I transferred to California, decided to hook up with a girl from his job, which turned out to be the real reason he couldn't move to be with me. No time to heal was ever taken between these relationships. I would just move on to the next, so inevitably, things fell apart.

Now, in a *situation-ship* with Larry, I found myself confronting yet another girl; "Well, as long as he keeps calling and saying what's up, I'm gone keep saying what's up!" Her snarky remark made me wish she were in the room so I could show her what was up. I knew it wouldn't be the end of things and that she wasn't the only one. The crazy part of this conversation is it was Myron's girlfriend (yes, the one he cheated with) conducting this interrogation for me as I listened on the other end. After this incident, I spiraled; if Myron hadn't cheated on me, I wouldn't be with LJ, and I wouldn't be dealing with all these other girls; but then again, my first love, Carlos had cheated too; so clearly there was something wrong with me, I had to be the problem, and I should just end it all now. I headed for the bathroom, grabbed whatever pills I could find, tossed them into my mouth, and took a huge gulp of water, but it was like my throat closed because I couldn't swallow a thing. I tried again, but still, it all just flowed back out. Throwing the pills and the open bottle of water across the room, I slid to the floor, weeping in complete surrender. For the third and final time, my attempt to end my life was thwarted.

A few months had passed, and I was sitting in the Emergency room staring at the nurse. I blinked absently as she waved her hand to bring me back to focus. "Hello, yes, you are pregnant." She repeated, this time it wouldn't be gossip. I was really going to be a mommy. The thought that went through my head was, how am I going to tell Myron, who wasn't even my child's father? I wondered how it would devastate him to share the news that I was having a baby with someone else so soon after we had broken up, but nothing prepared me for the reaction of LJ, the actual father. "Man, F*ck!" He yelled as he stormed into the bathroom and slammed the door behind him. I could hear muffled words and flying objects echoing from behind the door as I stifled my tears and thought, "He doesn't want us either, so what do I do now?" Suicide was **no longer** an option; I now had a child to live for.

The resounding words of truth, "Life for me ain't been no crystal stair," written in *Mother to Son*, a poem by Langston Hughes, plays repeatedly in my head like a broken record. I'd experienced love and endured its loss. I'd shared joyous moments and, of course, times of devastating events like you've already read and many others not mentioned in this brief synopsis. It was a year after the birth of my first child, while home from my mom's funeral, that I was cornered by my dad and his sister regarding my apprehensive behaviors towards him. With no way to escape, I had no choice but to let the cat out of the bag. Before fake news was in the media, I had been accused of reporting it. While my aunt told me I had made up his abuse of me, my dad was saying, "Well, I only wanted to show you what the boys would do to get in your pants." Shaking my head in disbelief, I allowed the tears to trickle and fall into the crook of my smile. I was crying, but it wasn't from pain. I was no longer bound by the opinions or ridicule of others. Those tears released negative pressure that had been intensely building within me. Three times, I had attempted to take my own life. While I had been saying that I failed at suicide, the reality is with all three attempts, I was shown favor, grace, and mercy.

God rescued me from the grave; now, my life is filled with light. **Job 33:28**

I was given a chance to live, and I was going to do it abundantly. My three children, Tristan, Aaiyden, and Alyssia, will never question my love for them nor feel as though they don't matter. My mindset was transformed, and I am no longer shaped and molded by the world around me or the actions of others. I have emerged from my cocoon as a beautiful butterfly that seeks and understands the word of God, El Roi (The God who sees me). If I ever feel discouraged, I remember my favorite bible verse: "For I know the plans I have for you, says the Lord, they are plans for good and not for disaster, to give you a future and a hope" Jeremiah 29:11.

Don't let what other people think about you determine how you feel about yourself; learn to know the love of God and believe you are enough.

My mindset was transformed, and I am no longer shaped and molded by the world around me or the actions of others.

— **Leona Elzy**

Independent Love

Salesha LOL

I thought about never getting married again, but after some deep thought, I changed my mind because I knew I was called to be a wife. Besides, I'm a Pisces, and we tend to be addicted to love. I also said I would never date long distances, but here I am, in a bi-coastal relationship 3,000 miles away. Although this new relationship has surprised me, it's honestly the best thing I've ever experienced. It's sure enough better than dating those local losers that belong in the toxic dating pool.

I'm the kind of person who lives out loud, which means I'm not afraid of transparency. Although most of the time, I don't want to, I share some things to give birth to hope in others. One day, I felt compelled to release a celebratory post on social media, but this time it was different. If I shared the post, I would be exposing that I was officially in an exclusive relationship. Even though I was hesitant, I obeyed that tug on my heart. I didn't share it for the results. I did it because, for one, God wouldn't leave me alone, and two, it was a way to remind myself that God took me from praying for it to walking in it. So, once I hit that post button, I was blown away. So many from my single ladies' tribe were smiling, clapping, and shouting with joy as they admired this news from afar. I'm grateful God decided to use me to provide that glimpse of hope because admiring black love was the exact hope I held onto by a thread during my single season. Suppose God has blessed me with the healthy, happy, and harmonious relationship I prayed for years for. In that case, He can do the same for others. But please understand that getting to this sweet spot wasn't smooth sailing. Let me take you down the pathway that led me to this prosperous place where I am today.

When I reached my mid-twenties, I went through some serious reflection. I realized that I was the black sheep of my family due to our generational history. My grandmother was married at twenty-two, my mother married at twenty-two, and my older sister also married at twenty-two. Then I turned twenty-two. Then I turned twenty-three. Then I turned twenty-four and Chile, by twenty-five, I just knew I had failed in life. God promised I would also be a wife, but it wasn't happening on time, or at least from what I thought the timing should look like. I wasn't privy to what a generational cycle breaker was or what that looked like. One day, I heard clearly from the Holy Spirit that it was my assignment to break this cycle before He would bless me with my heart's desire to have my own family. I became angry because why me? I became confused because this didn't seem like a bad family cycle. I was overwhelmed and afraid that I was too young and ignorant to carry out this mandate. Unfortunately, the guy I was dating didn't seem to value marriage like I did. He didn't understand why I was so adamant about getting married since he felt we were too young. So, once I turned twenty-six, I became like Sarah in the Bible and took matters into my own hands, but in the concept of marriage, of course. I was determined to grab the next man and marry him. Besides, dating wasn't working for me since I had no clue how to be a girlfriend or a single Christian. I didn't have a reference point for that growing up since most of my circle was married.

So, that next man was a friend I grew up with in church. Yep, a good 'ole church boy where our families already knew each other. This was safe, right? However, I did not consider that I did not know the current-day friend who grew into a man and had his own life experiences. Like many youngsters of age, I took the first chance I had to flee from the strict rules and ways of church. All my church friends and I split up, going our separate ways. Some went to college, some started families early or jumped into the workforce. However, this friend, who later became my husband, had a totally different plan for life that I had no idea about until I was warned by a phone call. The news I received was confirmed once this friend reappeared in my life by way of my mailbox. He couldn't show up in person as he was on an all-expense paid *trip* sponsored by the government and its taxpayers. A letter per day turned into multiple incoming phone calls per week, which then turned into multiple monthly visits. He returned home from his two-year *trip* on

A Piece Of Change

a Friday, and we were married that Monday, only a few weeks shy of me turning twenty-seven. Remember when I said I was determined? Even though I felt I was four years late, I felt obligated to get married by any means necessary. Because we were so young, dysfunctional, and inexperienced, things didn't take long to go downhill. My marriage started to feel forced and resulted in marital infidelity, financial infidelity, disrespect, and falling out of love.

2012 was the beginning of my cocoon season. This season felt like twelve long years of suffering, just like the lady in the Bible with the issue of blood. It started with me moving back home with my parents for a second time, but this time with a spouse. There were times he wouldn't come home for days and weeks at a time. He basically moved out without confirming it. He claimed he wanted to make up for the time he missed with his *family* while he was away. After months of going back and forth, we vowed to make things work, after he promised to attend marriage counseling and come back home. The Marriage Counselor asked him, *"Is there anything stopping you from moving forward in making your marriage work?"* He stated, *"No, that's why I'm here. I want to make things right."* I believed him, so we moved forward. That lasted maybe five months until he was right back out in the streets doing God knows what and with who. I got used to him being gone and having the bed all to myself. One night, while crying myself to sleep, the Holy

Spirit warned me that my marriage was going to end in death or divorce. At this point, I hated my husband, but I didn't want his life to end due to him being in the streets. Divorce wasn't my first thought since that was like a curse word in the traditional Baptist church. I prayed, released my worries, and moved on with life as a single-married woman. A few nights later, after attending a men's worship night, he came home unexpectedly to drop a bomb on me. He confessed that he was unfaithful and had brought a daughter into the world just a week prior and understood if I no longer wanted to be married. Welp, there was my confirmation, I was getting a divorce.

In October 2013, I put my husband out of the house again with confidence that this time, it was truly the end, and I could begin my healing, restoration, and self-discovery journey. That's when the cocoon shifted. It was dark, quiet, cold, and lonely. No sex. Yes, I said it! A total of eight years of abstinence. However, this was mostly by choice because I couldn't even fathom the thought of being with another man at that point. I went through some big ups that included completing my bachelor's degree and obtaining my Real Estate License just to discover I didn't like the Realtor life. I discovered my purpose by realizing that I'm better suited as a financial coach and housing advocate. With the big ups came some big downs and ugly moments, including losing multiple jobs, which left me feeling inadequate. I learned that dating after divorce was worse than before marriage. I had to heal through multiple breakups that destroyed my confidence. The ugliest part of this season was discovering that I had fun but fake friendships that made it hard for me to trust. Some of my closest friends, who were all married, showed their true colors by judging me for being a divorcee. It's sad that religion, unfortunately, can cause a wedge between those who are judgmental churchgoers and those who are Kingdom-minded. I had no support. No one to turn to for guidance on how to navigate this new life I was now forced to endure. Or so I thought in those moments. Thankfully, I was blessed with my B.E.T. (booked every Tuesday) family. This was a sisterhood that gathered every Tuesday night for bible study and inspirational book readings by a Virginia Beach Pastor who now leads the Restored Woman movement. I was so shocked to find out that many of them were also divorced and doing just fine in their new journeys. This gave me so much hope and peace.

Between my failed marriage and after-divorce dating experience, all the signs and red flags were there as an indicator that none of those men were right for me. However, like so many of us who crave love, I ignored the signs with hopes that they would somehow just magically disappear. This is dangerous as it often leads to ungodly soul ties. There was an occurrence where God commanded me to break a soul tie that I had on and off for seven years, before and after my marriage. However, I had no reference point back then to what a soul tie was or how to break it. This love, or at least what I thought was love, was like a drug. It was so hard to stop since it seemed so real. I learned that too much of the wrong *drug* can be deadly. My confidence, self-esteem, swag, and the ability to make sound decisions all died. It felt like my heart was ripped out of my chest and thrown into oncoming traffic like I was nothing. The mental and emotional abuse I encountered within those past relationships tore my heart to shreds, leaving me dripping in blood, sweat, and tears on the side of the road like a caterpillar to fend for myself. To heal, I had to go through the detox process, just like in the physical form of a true drug addict. This led to yet another shift in the cocoon.

Healing for me was forcing myself to look in the mirror to fall back in love with myself and embrace who I was becoming. That included several years of therapy; discovering my love to travel, both solo and blind traveling with a group of women who are now forever friends; solo dates to learn what I liked and didn't like; embracing self-care to ease the impact of the shift; daily gratitude journaling; reading devotions to deepen my relationship with God; learning hard lessons that everyone is not my friend; that I can't expect me from other people because it would lead to disappointment; that all money isn't good money; and that every door is not mine to walk through. It hurts to heal, but it's necessary.

In September of 2023, another shift occurred. "Okay God, I'm done! This dating game is ghetto, and I no longer wish to participate in dealing with unemotional, unhealed, and confused men who want me to chase them." I lifted my hands and surrendered my will for God's will as I recited the most real and raw prayer I've ever sent up to heaven. I recommitted to reading my prayer for my future husband again every day that I wrote during the Pandemic, after another horrible breakup. And what do you know, God showed me He heard me and that He has a sense of humor, too.

On October 19, 2023, I entered the first event of my 20-year class reunion with my bestie, and somehow, I got swept away by him. The man that God held in escrow for me all these years. For the rest of the night, I was engaged in hours of great conversation with him. From first grade through high school, he has always been the homie. No romantic chemistry or connection, and no acknowledgment that he was feeling your girl. Just homies that always had respect and love for each other. This was so weird and awkward for me since I was the only one in the room that seemed to be caught by my surprise. All eyes were observing and saying, oh yeah girl, he's coming for you! It took my bestie to say, "I'm going to give y'all some space because you are going to be Mrs. Mitchell." Assuming I had a confused look on my face, he pulled me closer to confirm her words were true and confessed his feelings that he held back for so long. *Wow, really, God?* But why reveal this now? If it was always supposed to be us, we could have started this journey years ago. At that moment, the Holy Spirit had to remind me of my surrender just a month ago and that His timing was perfect. Thank God for my ability to surrender because we've been inseparable ever since.

I believe good things take time and come to those who do not just wait but wait well. When you wait well, God can hide you in a cocoon and redeem time for you to prepare for the abundant life you deserve by releasing all the blessings he has stored up for you. Being in a cocoon season where God had to strip and rebuild me was the hardest but best thing ever! All the hard work of time, effort, sacrifice, migraines, losing weight like I was sick, tears, prayers, sowing seeds, and healing from past pain and trauma was so worth it because of the woman I've become in the process. I've learned to value real support and love of family, church family, true friends, and associates the way that they can give it. I've been blessed with a rewarding career and have new big dreams due to taking more risks and betting on myself.

So, as I'm writing this, I want to say that America may be celebrating Independence Day, however, I'm still celebrating my own personal Independence Day from being released from a toxic marriage. July 1, 2024, marked 10 years since my divorce was final. Now, years later, and in the last year of my 30s, it's time for me to break through and break free as a beautiful butterfly. Who would have thought that on the anniversary of my divorce, I would be flying across the country, hand in hand with the love of my life? I am not by any means a relationship expert or guru. However, for those who desire true love, peace, and contentment, I want to leave you with five pieces of change based on my experience.

#1 Get out of the toxic dating pool. No, like, for real. There's a whole ocean of love, so do not limit yourself to only your local surroundings. #2 Commit to your cocoon season and do not take anyone in there with you. That is your time to heal, develop, and grow. Outsiders will corrupt and prolong your process. #3 Develop a prayer life because prayer truly does change things. #4 Improve your health. When you look good, you feel good; when you feel good, you do good and make better decisions. It starts from the inside and shows up on the outside. So, be bold and try different foods. Besides, it takes a lot of energy to pursue true love. #5 Improve and maintain your finances. Not only does it please God to be a good steward over what he blesses you with, but this is crucial for a healthy relationship, especially if you are long-distance. If you are called to be a help mate but have jacked up finances, sis, how will you have the capacity to help him? Men, if you are called to be a provider for your future wife, how can she trust you to feel safe and secure if you can't even take care of yourself? I promise this is no shade because I have been on the financial struggle bus many times during my cocoon season and I'm still learning as I go. I may share that story one day. In the meantime, plenty of free resources are out there to help you get it together. Start with budgeting first. YouTube is your friend! As a bonus piece of change, be okay with being alone and open to what God has for you. It may not look like what you pictured, but I promise it will be even better and everything you need. Start your process of becoming the best version of yourself sooner rather than later and watch how your new independence attracts the real love you deserve and takes you by surprise.

Healing for me was forcing myself to look in the mirror to fall back in love with myself and embrace who I was becoming.

— Salesha LOL

My Reflection Unveiled
Michelle M. Hicks

I remember coming to Virginia from Missouri for Christmas. I saw changes in my mother but just chalked it up to her getting older. She was still making the best sweet potato pies, driving, and being the mother, I knew. I went back to Missouri after the holiday season and talked to her on the phone regularly. She would tell me what everyone was up to, who was doing good, and who was getting on her nerves.

My next visit, which was a few months later, was different. She was slowing down. Everyone was noticing, so we called a family meeting. My sister, brother (who lived with my mom), two nieces, and my daughter. We were concerned about her being alone for extended periods. My brother talked about her leaving food on the stove while cooking and never going back to check on it. We all agreed that she needed help. Mom was absent from our meeting but knew we were discussing her. She came from the back of the house and said, "I don't have cancer, and I don't need any help." We all looked at each other in amazement. Who knew anything about the *C-word*?

On the way back to Missouri this time, my husband and I were noticeably quiet. At some point in our drive, I looked at him, and he said, "I know. It is time to come back home."

I moved back to Virginia in January 2018. I came ahead of my husband. I needed to find a job and a place for us to live. I stayed with my mom. I watched her continue to do some things as normal, but other things were off. I found myself repeating things.

I took her to her next doctor's appointment. I had prepared myself for her not to know who I was. The doctor entered the room and asked, "Who do you have with you today?"

My mom responded, "My Daughter."

"What's her name?"

With a glance my way, my mom responded. "Michelle."

The doctor went on with the exam. When she had finished and released us to leave, I pushed my mom's wheelchair into the hallway and told the doctor that I had some concerns. I only heard her saying, "Your mom is very sick." Being paralyzed by her words, we left.

I continued to live with my mom while searching for a house. I thought I had found the perfect one. My husband contacted the realtor, and the ball was in motion. We were on our way to starting over in Virginia. After doing all we were supposed to do to get the house, we were told that we could not get it because it was tied up in some legal issues, so we went back to the drawing board. By this time, my husband had packed the house in Missouri and was here. Now, we are both living with my mom. That is a whole story all by itself.

Back to my mom.

I had to take her to another appointment that would change my life.

When the doctor asked me who I was, she said, "I don't know."

The doctor tried coaching her, "Is this your sister or your daughter."

My mom looked at me and asked, "Are you my sister or my daughter?"

"I'm your daughter."

The doctor chimed in, "What's her name?"

Mom responded. "I don't know."

Holding back tears, I said," I'm Michelle."

I had access to Mom's medical records, and after seeing them and seeing what the doctors had diagnosed her with, I googled it. Dementia is a condition characterized by progressive or persistent loss of intellectual functioning, especially with memory impairment and abstract thinking. The CDC defines multiple myeloma as abnormal plasma cells that build up in the bone marrow and form tumors in many bones of the body. I now know what the doctor meant when she said, "Your mom is very sick."

After dropping mom at her house, we had moved out at this point; I called my friend who had taken care of two parents who had dementia, this life-changing disease. As soon as she answered, I began my barrage of questions without warning. "Why didn't you tell me she would forget who I am." She allowed me to cry and rant, and when I finished, she empathized with me, "I'm so sorry."

How could my mom, the lady who always knew the right things to say, always supported, the mom who became a labor and delivery nurse, and the usher at the church, not know who her baby girl was?

Lord, how am I going to do all of this? Take care of my sick mother, husband, job, and church. I am overwhelmed by all of it! I do not have the strength! Then I hear in my spirit a familiar scripture, "My grace is sufficient for you, for my power is made perfect in weakness (2 Corinthians 12:9)."

Ugh. What does this mean? Now what? I realized that to understand what the Lord was saying and how I would process this, I had to read the whole chapter of 2 Corinthians 12 and look in the mirror to identify my weaknesses. Neither idea was appealing to me. I thought, is this the scripture that talks about a thorn in the flesh? And I know what looking in the mirror will do. It will cause me to look at me. I had to see the inner me to understand why I could not be what I needed to be for my mom.

I go to the mirror and scream. I do not like what I see. The person in the mirror was not *me*. Who is this broken, distorted-looking person? What in the world happened? The pain is all over my face. I wonder if anyone else could see it. Of course not. I have learned to mask it. And now I must reveal it to myself.

The mirror allowed me to speak to the Lord in a manner I have not done in years. I yelled at Him, "Why do I have to see my mom like this?" I was angry. I sat with my dad as he transitioned, and I do not know if I can do the same with my mom. It is not fair! I feel guilty when I do not get her to give my sister a break, and I hurt when I do. I am the baby of the family, and I have been trying to be a grown-up for years. I do not want to. I do not want to figure out what my mom is trying to say because she cannot remember the words. I do not want to bathe her because she cannot remember how.

I want my mommy back. I do not want to deal with my siblings! They are mean, and my mom is the buffer between us. When my mom was my mom, she handled them so I would not have to. And now you tell me to, "Glory in my infirmities?"

After the mirror, I read 2 Corinthians 12 again. What was I thinking? The mirror was rough, but the scripture revealed more of me I needed to see but did not want to deal with.

The me that I have been hiding behind in ministry. Teaching and preaching, healing and not being healed myself. Teaching and preaching wholeness when I am in pieces. These are the infirmities with which I must now deal.

Wait, God, are you telling me that my siblings are the thorn in my flesh? And you are having me deal with them so that I do not think I am better than them. But I never thought that I was. We all made decisions/choices. What are you really saying to me, Lord?

"Yes, you all made choices; theirs were out in the open, and yours were between you and your mom. She cannot remember them, but you know what they are. The same way you found Me in those times, Glory in your infirmities now. You know that if your mom comes to live with you, you will have nothing to do with your siblings. You only deal with them now because of your mom. Yes, they can be overbearing and even controlling at times, but they also have their stories to tell. I am allowing you to heal and be whole so that you can help them. I did not have to use your mom to do this, but I finally got your attention."

Man, the truth really does hurt. Now, I must take my own advice and "Heal." Just when I thought I was okay, God showed me the places of my brokenness. He showed me the dysfunction of my own self. The bondage that I am in is because I do not want to deal with the truth. It is the truth that will cause me to be free, but I must acknowledge it. It is not the truth as I see it, but the truth according to Him.

Why was I running from that conversation with The Father? I do not usually run from the truth. It is because I did not want to face the fact that I must change my mind concerning my siblings. It is easier not to deal with them. And now I must.

The mirror exposed my weaknesses, and the scripture revealed my infirmities. I left home in 1977 when I graduated from high school and went to college. Got married in 1980 and was gone for ten years. I stayed long enough to restore my relationship with God and was gone again. I do not really know my siblings as adults. I know what I saw when I came through town. I know what my mom would say when we talked. However, I do not know them and have not taken the time to get to know them.

I had to ask myself, "How can you be so patient with others and have zero tolerance for your siblings?" The answer I told myself was, "They should know better." They know the struggles of our mother and the addictions of our family members, and they choose to live like the hood that we grew up in. And once again, the Father shows HIS power. He Speaks, "Who are you to determine anything concerning your siblings or anyone else for that matter. The Grace that is sufficient for you is sufficient for them." Ouch.

Why did I have to look in that mirror? Why did I have to meditate on that scripture?

I realized that looking at that broken, distorted face showed me my weakness concerning my siblings. It showed me that I was grieving the loss of the mother that I once knew. The scripture showed me that I need to continue talking to the Father so that He could show me how to heal.

Even as I write this, I feel those invisible chains falling off. I am the one that allowed my relationship with my mom to change. This disease did not change my love. It showed me how much I loved her and what an honor it is to serve her.

I am learning to lean not to my own understanding but to a strength that is not mine. My weaknesses, my infirmities, the thorn in my flesh, are there so that I can obtain the strength I need to care for my mom. My siblings are who they are. I do not have to change who I am. I must know who I am and move on from there.

My weaknesses, my infirmities, the thorn in my flesh, are there so that I can obtain the strength I need…

— **Michelle M. Hicks**

Trials, Thorns, and Triumphs

Zaquinntia "Zee" Chamblee

I did not realize how vital it was not to have a father in my life. I needed advice and guidance as I navigated from childhood to adulthood. I often wondered why my father was not available for some of the most crucial times of my journey. I was often nervous when I was bullied by the kids in school and isolated from the other kids. I felt less than with no one to play with because the leader of the bullies told the other kids not to talk or play with me. I was alone and afraid; I would shake uncontrollably. I wanted to know where my father was when I was being chased home from school and beaten up. I suffered mental and physical abuse by a family member and the men in my life that led me to ongoing therapy today. I cried out to my dad to rescue me, but his help never arrived. I longed for his love, attention, and protection. After my peers called me ugly, I wanted to hear my dad say, "You are beautiful." I needed to talk about how a man should treat a woman. I yearned for my dad's protection when I was sexually assaulted by someone who claimed to love and adore me. I felt bad for my mother, who had to work long hours to support me, not knowing at the time that she was leaving me with my first abuser as a child. I wished my dad could have taken care of me, and I would not have experienced that torment. I felt so alone. I felt as though no one heard my cries for help. I had the bruises to prove it, but I hid them because of fear. The shame of being called "blackie, ugly, bumps and lumps" because of my acne, and "skinny pancake butt girl" made me feel unwanted. It had to be something wrong with me because my father did not want to take care of me, kids bullied and beat me, and my own flesh and blood had me on an emotional rollercoaster daily, showing love and care one day to calling me a whore and liar the next and I was just in elementary school when it started. All of them negatively shaped and molded my low self-esteem. The beatings, bruises, and painful words made me feel unattractive. Psalm 139:14 states I praise you because I am fearfully and wonderfully made; your works are wonderful; I know that full well. Although I read and meditated on this scripture as an adult, I still found it hard to process because I never heard my earthly father call me beautiful. I poured out my soul in my first poem about love in the ninth grade. I felt that no one really cared about my writing, but it always made me feel better after putting my feelings on paper. For the first time, I felt a sense of accomplishment when my love poem was displayed in the front entrance case with the other kid's accomplishments alongside the school's trophies of my school. I really hoped for congratulations. When I performed in the concert and marching band, why didn't I see my father in the stands alongside the other fathers? During my first marriage, I had to receive an emergency Csection, which was terrifying for a young mother who had never had surgery before. This was another terrifying moment in my life while I lay cut open, bringing life into the world, not knowing if I was going to live or die because the doctors had a challenging time waking me from the anesthesia. I remember the abuse from my husband and thinking, here is another man who does not value my existence. I gained enough courage to divorce my first husband when my kids were toddlers. I did not know how I was going to take care of them alone, but I realized I was taking care of them alone anyway because my husband was never home. He was out cheating on me, another slap in the face. I was unworthy of love. I hate to admit it, but I was jealous of other people who had their dads actively in their lives and created lasting memories to be shared and passed from generation to generation. I loved and admired my dad, although I did not think he deserved it. But my mother raised me to love everyone, but I did not have to like their behaviors. I began to think something was wrong with me because my biological father was never present at such pivotal moments in my life. I had bad relationships with men, which led to three divorces. I began to realize this was a pattern. These were trials that God allowed me to go through to strengthen me. The men that were in my life were not emotionally available for me because they were not emotionally stable from what I now know because they suffered abandonment issues as well, and you cannot give what you do not have. I asked and pleaded with God to remove whatever it was in me that caused men to be unavailable to me throughout my life. Although God removed their presence, He did not remove the thorns I felt sticking to me throughout my life. It felt like this dark void had a tight grip on my entire being, leaving a gaping hole in my heart. My toiling in the pit had been pure torture, but I had hoped that one day, my life would change, although I would still carry the thorn of the feeling of abandonment. But I knew God had a ram in the bush for me, and eventually, I received the help I needed to somewhat maneuver through life. In the book of 2 Corinthian 12:7, it states [though Paul begged and wanted the thorn removed and did not see it as a gift, which the gift was God's grace, and it is enough; it is all we need.] Although men played a key role in my abandonment issues and were never available for me, I must bear the remembrance of abandonment to continue to learn and remember from it so that I will recognize the significance of my personal thorn, and that significance is to help others manage their ways through their trials and thorns to reach their triumphs in their lives to pay it forward and help others that God puts on their paths.

As an adult with two children to raise, I remember when my dad became deathly ill and did not tell me. I still showed compassion, care, and love; I made time to be available for a father who was never available to me. It was heart wrenching to find out that my dad was ill from a cousin who delivered the message so casually, like giving me the forecast for the week. To find out that he was using drugs and became infected with the HIV virus disturbed me tremendously. I never knew he was using and addicted to drugs. After finding out where my dad was, I immediately jumped in my car and went to him. I heard a whisper in my ear saying, "He never came to your rescue, but you are going to his." When I opened the front door to my grandmother's house and saw him lying there covered with blankets, his eyes sunk in, and to see his frail body when the last time I saw him, he was tall, dark, muscular, and handsome; it hurt me to the core to see him in that condition. I remember asking "Why didn't you tell me you were sick?" Well, his response was disheartening. He responded with, "I thought someone else in the family would have told you by now." I was no longer the little girl who was afraid to speak up. I remember raising my voice at him, "It was not their responsibility to tell me. It was your responsibility." I felt unworthy again because I felt that even on his deathbed, I was not good enough or important enough for him to ask someone to give him a phone so that he could tell me himself. I am embarrassed to say this, but at that very moment, he was a coward. Although he was sick, I was angry with him. I thought to myself, yet again this man is hurting me. I thought that he was selfish for not telling me about his deadly health condition. This was serious! It was not like he had the common cold and would get better in a few days. He was dying and made me feel guilty because I could not do more to help. How ironic is that? I felt that he should have been the one hurting through the past years because he was incognito. I realized that this has been his response to me all my life. He ran and ignored accountabilities and responsibilities. I was angry with him because he robbed me of a life with a father. Yet, I did not turn my back on my dad. I was a struggling single mother at the time, working a full-time job and not making a lot at the time, but whatever he asked me for, I made sure he had it. I was stressed, depressed, sad, heartbroken, and tired from work but I visited him every day until he passed away. I was happy to hear him finally tell me that he loved me and not that I did not believe him, but I only wished that he would have shown me through the years instead of me always questioning where he was. He never had to ask, "Where were you?" When I was told about his sickness, I was there for him; I followed through. After he passed, I asked God "Where is my earthly father?" I was in so much pain. I was confused. I wanted to know if my earthly father asked my heavenly father for forgiveness and if he was going to be accepted into heaven. I never received a response from God.

God protected me and gave me the endurance to get up every day and never give up. As life continued to pass, I understood and appreciated going through the slaps, shoves, punches, verbal, mental, and physical abuse. I began to understand my plight in life. That plight is to help others and to go through the actual experiences so that I would have genuine empathy for others. I am thankful that my Heavenly Father guided me throughout my childhood and adulthood. He was with me through the bullying, the mental, emotional, and physical abuse; none of it killed me, it made me stronger. I had to go through life's trials, and carry my thorns, so that I would be ready to boldly receive and walk into my triumphs that God had waiting specifically for me, and there were many. I want to present my testimony and to share my triumphs so that others can see that it is possible to get trampled on through life and still enjoy a life transformed from the most painful blows to the heart to the most pleasing and blissful moments to the soul. By going through the hardships, I learned and became aware of my purpose, and that is to advocate for those who have gone through similar experiences. The trials and thorns hurt, but they led me to many triumphs in my life. Through the trials and thorns, my triumphs have been vast. Through the pain, shame, feeling less than others, I was still able to graduate with a BS degree in Human Services with distinction, a certification in Addiction Prevention and Treatment, a Qualified Mental Health professional T A/C, and acceptance into Grad School majoring in Counseling (MSED/EDS) concentration in Clinical Mental Health Counseling, and finally a writer.

I also found out that another close loved one of mine has a drug addiction and is HIV positive. This one ripped through my soul; the pain was intense. I found myself asking God again why, and I finally received the answer. Because of my loved ones' addictions and diseases, I found myself wanting to help people who are battling addictions that lead them to mental and physical illnesses. I wanted to understand addictions so that I could help save lives. Looking back, would I change anything? I will say no because I would not have gained the strength and courage to live out my dreams and goals. I could not change any of the situations that I went through anyway because it was all a part of God's script for my life. I went through the peaks and valleys, and although challenging, I have soared, and I am not done yet. There is much work to be done and I do not want my trials or thorns to be in vain. I will continue to assist others who are asking the same question I asked for years but instead of looking to man for the answers, I have shared with others to look to God for all answers, even if it takes years to receive answers…do not give up. The most rewarding commodity is how my Heavenly Father utilized my earthly father in molding me into the woman I have become today. In essence, by my dad not being involved in the different stages of my life's journey, he contributed in helping me grow and mature, becoming a woman who does not give up even in the absence of a man who I thought I could not make it in life without, when the absolute truth is it only pushed me closer to the one who protected me, guided me, listened to me, provided for me, and most importantly loved me enough to always be near and I never have to ask my Heavenly Father, "Where are you." God was always with me, and allowed horrific things to happen to me, but it was to equip me to take care of His people. *Though he slay me, yet will I hope in him; I will surely defend my ways to his face.* ~Job 13:15 NIV~

I want to present my testimony and to share my triumphs so that others can see that it is possible to get trampled on through life and still enjoy a life transformed from the most painful blows to the heart to the most pleasing and blissful moments to the soul.

— Zaquinntia "Zee" Chamblee

Stepping Away from Safety

Renita D. Harris

"Do not be afraid or discouraged, for the Lord will personally go ahead of you. He will be with you; he will neither fail you nor abandon you." I am walking in my prayers from years ago. Everything I currently have is what I prayed for. These were my prayers, and now I pray that God teaches me how to steward all He has provided. It sounds good now, but it took tears, prayers, and patience to get where I am.

In June 2003, I sat in a dark bedroom with an energetic six-year-old and a crying four-month-old. I silently cried, promising myself that I must make a change for these girls. I never want my kids to experience life as I did. They deserve better. *God, please help me was always my prayer.* Their dad was present in the home but not as active. We were a family, but I was the sole provider in all aspects. I cooked, played, and was emotionally there for them, and I grew so tired. I knew that God was going to provide, but I was just not sure when He would show up. I had to put a plan in place to figure out how I could make things better for my daughters and me, so I enrolled in school. I sat in that bedroom caring for two kids; one child was running around and jumping on beds, and the other kept crying as their dad played his game.

We were young and learning there was no manual, but this was my family. July, it's time to go back to work. I worked an early shift starting at four in the morning. I'd leave home at 3 a.m. to drop my baby off at my mother's and then head to work after. My oldest daughter was at home with their dad, and he sent her off to school because he worked in the neighborhood as a maintenance technician. One night, my babies and I were lying in the dark bedroom trying to sleep, and their dad was out with his friends for the evening. I heard rambling at my window. Our neighborhood was quiet, and there was little crime, but this sudden rambling startled me. I got out of bed with the phone in my hand, walking through the dark room towards the window. As I opened the blinds, I saw someone dressed in all black, a gun in their hand, and a second person breaking into my car. I banged on the window and ran. Instead of calling the police, I called the kid's dad, screaming," Please come home. Someone just broke into my car; I'm ready to move; I can't raise my kids like this."

I felt violated; I had to find a new home for us, so I settled for a home closer to my parents. With this move, we went through a loss of employment, financial struggles, and heartaches. We matured, we grew up, and then we grew apart. In December 2009, I received a phone call from a familiar voice that startled me due to their crying. "Baby, the girls." I was confused, so I asked, "What's wrong? The girls are right here with me." The voice sobbed even harder,

A Piece Of Change

saying, "No, the other girls, I can't keep this secret any longer. He has two other girls, and they live with me." My heart sank. Did I hear this correctly? On Christmas Eve, I learned that the man I have a family with has two younger daughters. I hung up. I felt betrayed, heartbroken, and very frustrated. I wanted to scream, but I went into the room, cried, got myself back together, and went back into mommy mode, allowing my kids to enjoy Christmas. I started to feel like I was the problem because this was not the life I wanted for my kids. I grew depressed for days. I wept in the shower to mask the emotional turmoil I was feeling. I needed to set a better example for my daughters. I needed my girls to see a better version of me. I knew that I had to walk away from this relationship because it was no longer healthy for me. Life had to be better than this. I couldn't keep living in depression and being deceived. I started to pray more, and I started attending church weekly. I needed to be grounded spiritually, and I needed to plan my next move away from this home. I saved money when I could, and I eventually found an apartment in a new city that was still close to my parents; I moved to Chesapeake, VA, and I decided this move didn't include their dad because he was part of the change that I needed.

On a sunny Saturday morning in March, the move was here. I called my sister and a few friends; we packed up a moving truck and moved my belongings to my new apartment. We made three rounds of loading and unloading. On round three, everyone was tired, so we lay on the vacant floor, planning what needed to be loaded on the last move. As we did, we heard a car arrive and commotion outside. I walked towards the door, and my kid's father appeared in the doorway. Visibly upset, he asked, "So you really were going to move and not tell me?" At that moment, I expressed to him that I was tired of trying, tired of being disappointed, and ready to try life a different way. Although upset, he understood that we had tried to make the relationship work but were not successful. He helped us make our final move and gathered his belongings, which I packed up and placed in boxes.

This point of change in my life is tough because I walked away from a relationship that I knew no longer served me purpose. I finally chose to be happy and obedient even during hard times. At this new apartment, my daughters and I started to build inseparable bonds that couldn't be broken. I worked full-time, attended school part-time, and still had to be a mother. Life was happening around us. There were struggles; we lost family members, and we lost friends, but we kept our smiles. There were days we barely had enough, but the girls never knew we were lacking, and I made sure they never missed out on opportunities. I also started to hate my job. I had been in a call center for over ten years and was burned out. I desired a career, and every day before entering the office, I sat in the parking lot and I would cry out to God, "Lord, please open doors that are greater. Please open doors for my career." One day, things felt different; it was very somber, and everyone had their heads down. I led a team of ten call center agents, so it wouldn't be long before one of them came to my desk. As soon as my computer loaded, I received a call from my boss asking me to go to the conference room. It was quiet, and there sat four individuals with sad looks on their faces. As soon as the door shut, I heard, "Renita, there's a lot of change going on with the company. We suffered a lot of financial loss, and today, we must lay you off effective immediately." I, along with three other managers, were let go. I walked out of that office with what felt like a weight lifted off my shoulders. When I got to my car, I knew that God was answering my prayers, but I had to truly trust Him.

With being laid off, this is when true transformation started to happen for me. I did receive a severance package, but I needed to figure out life because I still had to live and take care of my kids. I focused on obtaining employment and excelling in school. I was unemployed for ten months. I lost faith, and I got discouraged, but I managed to hide the frustration and keep a smile on my face. I had to continue to trust and believe that things would get better. I had no job and little to no money in my bank account, but I never stopped smiling. My kid's father stepped up, providing tremendously for the girls, and our mothers both helped when needed. I knew God wouldn't let me down. This was a faith walk. As I continued to lose the little bit of faith that

I had and depression sank in, I stopped attending school, and all I wanted was to get a job. My sister worked at a local shipyard, which made me aware of an open role within the human resources department. Although I didn't have any experience in Human Resources, I applied and hoped that my resume would get in the right hands. Being unemployed helped transform me into the woman I am today, and I was ready for change.

It was the middle of the day, and the girls were at school. I was in a dark bedroom in silence as my phone rang. On the other end was a manager from the shipyard. She stated, "I received your resume; I see you don't have any human resources experience, but the previous work you have done is transferable; I would like to interview you." I hung up with full confidence that God was in the midst of this. I prayed, cried, and I claimed this position as mine. I went to the interview well-prepared, and three weeks later, I started my first role in Human Resources. I walked into this role, claiming I would have new opportunities and new goals, and I thanked God for opening this door for me. I met new people working here. There was one person I know God strategically placed to help push me out of my funk and push me to want more. She would encourage me to enroll in school, saying, "Renita, you are raising daughters who are looking up to you, so set the example for them." I reenrolled in school, and unbeknownst to me at the time, I only had two semesters remaining to receive my degree. This news made me excited, and I sat down with my kids to let them know that we had to stay focused for the next eight months so that I could complete school. I went to work, went to class, attended soccer practice and games for one child, and then praise dance at church for the other. There were days I would take my daughter to church for dance and then head to a coffee shop nearby to complete class assignments. While in a marketing class, I would often hear about a major consulting firm that took great care of its employees. I used to say, "God, I would love to work for this company," but I didn't know accounting, nor did I have any consulting experience, so I knew this was just a dream, but I still asked God to make it happen.

It was time for graduation, and I knew that having this degree would open doors for me. My family traveled to watch me graduate, and I felt so happy to have my babies watch me as I received my bachelor's degree. Immediately after graduation, I was offered a role as a Campus Recruiter for a government contractor, and I knew this was the start of the transition I had hoped for. I worked hard day and night, and I traveled to colleges. Some days, I recruited college students, and things were now falling into place. My kids were maturing, and my oldest daughter was heading to her first year of college. My youngest daughter kept me busy with dance classes, and I also built a solid friendship with the girl's father. I was able to be a friend and co-parent to him, and that alone helped tremendously. Their dad was a provider, and when I said the girls needed anything, he made sure they had it. One day, he called and said that he had just talked to our oldest daughter and that he wanted our youngest and me to meet him for dinner. We had dinner, they played together, and then we parted ways. He told us that he loved us and walked away. That next morning, as I was sitting at my desk working, his mother called, crying. I could not understand what she was saying, but the call disconnected. I called back, and there was no answer; I then called his aunt, and she calmly said, "Baby, he is gone. He was murdered." A sharp pain hit the pit of my stomach, and I could not move. I messaged my coworker and calmly told her I had to go. As the room spun, all I could think about was my daughters. "How do I tell them that their dad is no longer here?" My friend stepped in, and she gave my coworker her address; no one wanted me to drive in a state of shock. Meanwhile, my friend went into action, instructing my brother to pick up my oldest from college. As we waited for her arrival, she coached me for what felt like hours. She said, "Renita, you can cry it out now, but when the kids get here, you dry your tears and stand strong for your daughters because they need you." It hurt living in that season, the trial, the grief, the sentencing, and still grieving. I had to lean on God for strength. I was living in a dark season during that time. I questioned God, I cried, but I found strength and knew I had to do all that I could to make sure my daughters had all that they needed, with me now being their only surviving parent.

I started working so hard and was flourishing; I needed my girls to see me work hard and accomplish goals. I was recognized at work for being a top performer and promoted multiple times, and now I was ready to purchase my first home. I knew this was a huge step. My daughters and I were driving down the street, and we saw a nice new condominium development. We viewed an open model; as we walked through the spacious home, the exterior was red, and the inside was all we needed, with three bedrooms and two and a half bathrooms. I went back to the sales office and completed the application, hoping for approval. Days went by, and no response from the realtor; then I received an email saying the loan was denied. I was discouraged, but I sat down with my kids, and I told them we did not get approved for the home. My oldest daughter reminded me that God would move for us when it was time. She said, "It's just not our time, and it will happen when God is ready; let's just buy decorations and store them for when it is our time."

Life kept going. My daughters and I kept growing together. I decided to start the home-buying process without a house in mind, and I received a preapproval to buy a home from. Days after receiving the preapproval, the home I visited two years ago, which was denied, was now in foreclosure. I prayed, "God, I trust you. If this is you, please make the process easy." I contacted my realtor and asked to view the home. As we walked through the home, the girls eagerly claimed their rooms, and I noticed that the home only needed paint and new carpet. I fell in love with this home all over again, so I made an offer, and it was accepted. I purchased a three-year-old home for $150,000 less than what it was when I previously viewed it. I cried, and I thanked God for opening this door. It was God's timing.

We have all moved in, and we love the home and the neighborhood. I worked hard, and now I have started to desire more in my position at work, but I didn't know where else the role could take me. I felt like I was stuck because there was no way to advance. I started to apply for open roles, and I noticed a role with a major consulting firm that I dreamt of working for. I prayed and asked God, "Lord, if this position is meant for me, make it easy." I received a job offer from the company that I prayed for years ago. I am walking in the prayers I asked God for a home, and in the career I prayed for, and He answered my prayers.

I've been transitioning and changing for years now. I trust there is so much greater in store for me. As I transformed throughout life, I learned that some people and places could not go with me on this journey. I tried to hold on to relationships that were no longer healthy, I tried to keep a job that was causing me so much stress, and once I truly let go of these things, I started to find peace.

I would tell anyone that life gets hard, but when there are things that no longer serve your purpose and are no longer healthy, let them go. When you are in a season where you feel like life is getting the best of you, you must learn to trust the process and remember never to give up. At any given moment, you have two options: step back into safety or step forward into change.

As I transformed throughout life, I learned that some people and places could not go with me on this journey.

— Renita D. Harris

I'm Finally A Butterfly

Princess Barnes

It is 2024, and I am living my best life, especially to the people on the outside looking in. I am a veteran, wife, mom, grandmother, daughter, sister, aunt, and serial entrepreneur. I am a seven-figure earner, own a big house, several luxury cars, jewelry, and several rental properties, and travel the world. Many view my life as perfect. The truth is that I hold so many titles, and that leads to me having to be everything for everyone. I love my life, but if I am being honest, this shit gets exhausting.

I'm beyond grateful to be living because I was not living in my truth years ago, and I developed a hatred for myself. I had so many conversations with myself, trying to talk myself out of the darkness. Everyone thought I had it all together. I was becoming increasingly successful. They had no clue that I was slowly drifting away. The only people that knew something was off were my children and husband.

Growing up, I always felt like I had to be the best; even when I was the best, it was still not enough. Some years ago, I realized that my parents' separation led to this need to be the best; I subconsciously believed that my being the best would keep people around. Oh, was I wrong. In fact, it was the total opposite.

I fucked myself up. I competed with myself. When competing with others, you learn to accept losing at some point, but competing with yourself leaves no room for defeat. Every time I took what I considered to be a loss, a little piece of me died. I was in a damn battle with myself; I was my worst enemy.

I developed a fear of winning; I know it sounds ridiculous. I never had a large circle, but once I began to accomplish the goals that I set for myself, the circle turned into a dot. That mindset of being the best to keep people around shifted. I felt as if I was being punished for doing better.

Losing the relationships that I had was painful, but I was not willing to shrink. Why should I have to? If they loved me, they should have been cheering for me instead of separating. I struggled for a long time with them; was it me? Eventually, I figured it out and realized we were just on different paths.

It took me some time and a whole lot of unwanted problems to get here. I was suffering from impostor syndrome; Even when I was winning, I was losing because I honestly believed that I did not deserve it. I was living a double life; I still had to be the best, but I did not want anyone to know about my success. Being the best meant that I had to strive for self-improvement and personal growth in many aspects of my life. I had to continuously improve my skills, knowledge, relationships, and well-being.

By 2013, I had accomplished success in some parts of my life. I earned a bachelor's degree, and I started a business. I was in my third year of marriage, and everything was going great. I finally had a grasp on life, so I thought. I neglected the most important thing that needed to be the best: my well-being.

Focusing on my children, husband, and business was my main priority. I gave all of me to their well-being by any means necessary. If I could continue to get up and do what was needed, I would be good. As the days went on, it became challenging to do what was needed. I did this for years, ignoring all signs that something was wrong. I broke in 2017.

I was battling several mental health disorders that I was diagnosed with in 2015, including bipolar disorder, anxiety, panic disorder, and depression, and I was drinking every day to cope. In my mind, I was not worthy of success, and I honestly felt like a fraud. I had convinced myself I did not deserve any achievements because I was crazy. At least, that is what society thinks. I did my best to keep my problems to myself, shit, my husband did not even know.

I was seeing a therapist, but I still refused to accept my diagnosis; I was sneaking into treatment. I was just going through the motions, and I was not putting anything to use that I was learning. I refused to believe that I had these problems because people with these issues cannot function properly, according to society. How will I run my business?

Who would trust my judgment? The questions were endless, and I refused to risk my livelihood.

I had people depending on me; I had to be strong for them. My admitting that I had these problems would have made me feel weak. So, I decided it was best to manage it on my own. I have always managed things on my own. This could not be that much different; I was wrong. This was one of the hardest things I have had to face. It almost took me out.

They saw the drastic mood swings, and I became withdrawn. I loved my family, but I hated myself more, so in an effort to hide my truth, I chose to distance myself. This only piled on more problems, and now my marriage was suffering. At this point, I was like, to hell with it all; I felt as if I just could not win.

Most people would have said pray about it, but I was prayed out; I felt like God was no longer interested in my problems. Truthfully, I blamed him for everything; he made me crazy; he allowed my parents separation, and the list goes on. It got to the point that I did not care if I went to bed and did not wake up. I was completely exhausted and did not have any fight left in me.

I would look in the mirror and see my face, but I no longer recognized the reflection; my eyes were different. One day, I stood in the bathroom mirror looking at myself, something I had avoided for some time, and I saw the pain in my eyes. I had a conversation with the reflection I saw. The first thing

I said was, "You are better than this!" I said it repeatedly; I still can taste the salt from the tears flowing down my face. This was the first time in an exceptionally long time that I truly believed what I was saying about myself.

I made up my mind that I no longer wanted to be a prisoner and that I wanted to live. I was ready to live in my truth; I was tired of being an impostor. The fear of winning drowned out the fear of losing. This time, I wanted and needed desperately to win my life back.

The first thing I had to do was be honest and accept that I had some problems that I needed to work on. The hardest part was telling my husband that damn fear started creeping back in. I was afraid that once he knew about all my mental disorders, he would leave with my children. My thought process was that people would leave me when I was doing good, and he would leave because I was far from good.

One night, we were lying in bed in total darkness, and he was at what I believe to be his breaking point. He was venting about our relationship and wanted answers; I was all out of excuses. Even though I was upset with God, I asked him to give me strength. I was finally ready, and he showed up! Tears filled my eyes and started pouring out like a too-full glass of water. I took a deep breath and opened my mouth; everything came out. I told him about my diagnosis. I let him know about my secret therapy sessions. I felt fear, relief, shame, disbelief, and happiness, but the best feeling was freedom.

I can't tell you that everything was all peachy because it wasn't, but I can tell you that things made a turn for the better. My marriage no longer felt strained, and I even told my children that the whole house now had a better understanding of me. They were able to remove the thought that they were the problem, and I was able to be myself. I had finally made peace with all of me.

I realized that I was working so hard to be someone else because I did not want to accept who I am that I almost lost everything, including my life. I am who I am meant to be; this is and will always be me. I am not perfect, but I am perfectly made.

I decided to believe and trust that God never put more on us than we can manage. This journey has not been easy, but it is definitely doable. I thought living a normal life would be impossible until I defined my own normal. Regularly seeing a therapist is a huge and important part of my life. I am living on my terms and enjoying every second.

Living my life unapologetically has freed me from society's standards of normality. I'm no longer stressed about what people may say. Doing what works for me is now my priority. Sometimes, that looks like a few days in bed, laundry undone, racing to complete deadlines, etc. That is okay because I'm finally comfortable in my skin.

I am no longer an impostor; I am living in my truth. I can operate in my purpose, no longer hiding my achievements.

There is no longer a dark cloud following me around. Do not get it twisted; there are still rainy days. When those days come, I remind myself that the sun will always shine again.

Developing coping skills to help me along this journey was and still is essential. I have accepted that this is my forever journey, and I refuse to get lost along the way. It is not all bad, despite what some may think; it has made me a better person all around. I'm not saying that I am Perfect Patty, but I do my best to give grace; you never know what others are dealing with.

I have had some people say that mental illness is not of God; they believe it can be prayed away. Those people can kiss where the sun does not shine. I cannot speak for anyone else, but God was not answering my prayers on this matter. Until I realized that this required more than prayer; it required me to get the treatment I needed, try modern medications, and I had to put in the work.

I am sure you are thinking, why would you be okay with living like this? Of course, I was not at first, but let me be frank: I only had two options, and that was to choose to live or die. I could have given up long ago; instead, I chose to live. My choosing to live has allowed me to be here for my family and work in my purpose.

Two of my companies service individuals who have intellectual disabilities, physical disabilities, and some also suffer from mental health. . I am able to advocate and be their voice when they can't. I feel I can truly relate to our individuals, which allows me to provide adequate care. So, something that I viewed as a curse is actually a blessing.

I am a better leader as well; I am able to see beyond the surface. I encourage communication, and I push mental health breaks. My past and my disorders have prepared me for leadership. You must possess empathy and sympathy when leading others.

My family dynamics are great, we have open communication. My husband and I encourage our children to be themselves no matter what others think. They understand the importance of mental health days. They're thriving, healthy, and happy, and they have a mother who has mental disorders.

My husband and I just celebrated our fourteenth wedding anniversary, and we are still very much in love. He gets me, and I get him; we are definitely each other's person. We push one another when necessary, and he does not allow me to visit the darkness too long.

If someone had told me a few years ago that I would be in this space in my life, I would have tried to put my hands on them. I would have taken it as they were being sarcastic because all I saw was the end; the future did not exist for me. I am so grateful to be able to be in the space of acceptance, truth, love, happiness, and the list goes on. It is evidence that anything is possible, despite what it looks like.

If you are reading this and you are suffering in silence, you don't have to. Get help! You can get through this by surrounding yourself with the right people. I am proof that mental illness does not have to be the end. You can live in your truth and be the best version of yourself. You are the author of your story; you're in control.

As for the people in the back who are always judging others, check yourself. You never know what a person must do in order to survive or how close they are to breaking. Do not be the cause of someone breaking. If you cannot or do not want to help, please do not hurt.

Honestly, there have been blessings on top of blessings. So many doors opened once I accepted my truth. I have done public speaking and written two books so far, and my businesses are thriving. It is as if God is saying, now you're ready. I cannot believe that I expected God to trust me with certain things when I did not even trust myself.

What I deal with is not a quick fix. Every day does not feel good; I still have moments when I doubt myself. I'm getting through this, and I will continue to cope. I will never overcome my illnesses unless God says otherwise. Sometimes I can't drive, I have sleepless nights, I'm anxious a lot, my appetite comes and goes just like my weight, I'm an overthinker, etc. I am now completely okay with that. I am different!

Being different is not a bad thing. It means that you stand out from the crowd and have unique qualities that make you special. Rather than trying to fit in with the norm, we should embrace our individuality and celebrate what makes us different. Embracing and celebrating our differences is an important part of creating a society that values diversity and inclusivity.

Strive to become the best version of yourself by embracing challenges, learning from mistakes, and adapting to new situations. Focus on developing your strengths, overcoming your weaknesses, and being true to your values and beliefs. Learn to accept the things you cannot change but change what you can when necessary.

The idea that we all possess superpowers challenges the traditional notion of heroism. It suggests that anyone can be a hero, regardless of their background or circumstances. By embracing our inner strength and potential, we can achieve remarkable things and make a positive impact on the world.

I now genuinely believe that the world needs me and that I'm a hero in my eyes and in someone else's.

I now genuinely believe that the world needs me and that I'm a hero in my eyes and in someone else's.

— **Princess Barnes**

Fly Butterfly Fly

I have no idea what comes next. I don't know where I'm going, but I am equipped to journey wherever my wings take me. You see, I didn't always look like this, but what you have witnessed is the death of what was and a rebirth of what is. I represent the journey of self-discovery and the ability to change and evolve. I am God's beautiful manifestation of what it looks like to be transformed.

What I've learned is that I don't have to know where I'm going. I'll quietly land here or there for a moment but as you attempt to capture where I've landed, my wings have taken me to my next destination. It doesn't matter where I am; the important thing is that my wings remain in a position to fly at a moment's notice. I'm free and beautiful, and I have been released from uninvited, unfair, and sometimes self-inflicted suffering. I'm consciously awakened and aware of my resilience. As a symbol of change, I represent significant life changes and the ability to endure challenging moments.

The transformation was slow and difficult at times, but my amazing metamorphosis is nothing short of inspiring. My delicate beauty is something to behold. As I spread my wings, it is a reminder of the infinite possibilities of my transformation. Beloved, allow my wings to serve as a potent reminder of life's transformative moments and our innate capacity to evolve and transcend.

With just my piece of change, I'll spread my beautiful wings and soar as I follow the mandate that all butterflies are given, and that is to… FLY, BUTTERFLY FLY!

About The Authors

Ifedayo Greenway

Ifedayo is a mother, speaker, and master life coach.

She is the CEO of IG & MORE LLC. As a transformational coach, Ifedayo produces an annual event, *The Change Experience,* which empowers women to embrace their personal change journey.

She is the founder of the *She Unveils* movement, where she serves and helps others accomplish their literary goals by unveiling, writing, and publishing their stories. She has been featured in Huffington Post, CBS, FOX, NBC, and Shoutout Atlanta for her literary works (*Removing The Face & Removing The Fear*).

Ifedayo is a nine-time author and four-time best-selling author. Four of those books are collaborations where she serves as the Visionary Author. In addition to her books, she has also published inspirational writings and articles that have reached thousands of readers in various mediums, including Thrive Global & Faith Heart Magazine.

Ifedayo is passionate about her covenant with God to impact the world & uses her journey to strengthen & encourage women to find their authentic voice in their pursuit of transformation.

Connect with Ifedayo at: www.igandmore.com

Sonya the SheE.O

Sonya, the "She-E.O", is dedicated to guiding others through life's challenges with grace and tenacity. Born and raised in Richmond, VA, her journey is a testament to the strength of the human spirit. She navigated the complexities of life, from the hardships of being a prison wife to the heartbreak of divorce, emerging stronger and more determined than ever.

Driven by her unwavering commitment to helping others, Sonya founded a nonprofit organization dedicated to supporting returning citizens from prison and their families. As an author, her words resonate deeply with readers, illuminating the path to personal growth, resilience, and self-love.

With a heart full of compassion and a spirit that knows no bounds, Sonya continues to uplift and empower individuals from all walks of life. Her message is clear: no matter the obstacles, there is always hope, and within every individual lies the power to overcome and thrive

Connect with Sonya at: Sonya@sonyathesheeo.com

Angela N. Jackson

Angela was born and raised in Richmond, Virginia, and moved to North Carolina in 2007. She is a mother, grandmother, and a licensed foster care provider. Her mission is to be an inspirational role model for kids going through tough times, providing them with the support, hope, and encouragement they need to know things will get better. Angela is a proud HBCU (Johnson C. Smith University) alumna with a degree in Business Administration. Her current position as a Social Worker has enabled her to assist families that require support in regaining their social and economic independence. She is active in her community and enjoys traveling, cooking, and listening to the smooth sounds of Rhythm & Blues. She believes that everyone can contribute to improving the state of this world by showing love, compassion, and the will to help others.

Connect with Angela at: angie.jaxson@yahoo.com

Mendy Huff

Mendy was born and raised in Newark, New Jersey where she met her husband Dwayne they have been married for 36 years! They have 4 adult daughters. As a military spouse of over 30 years, Mendy has served as an Ombudsman as well as taken an active role in various Military Spouse Groups including serving as an advisor and mentor.

Mendy is passionate about empowering, inspiring, and encouraging women to put their best face forward in life and career.

Connect with Mendy at: mendyhuff@gmail.com

Reverend Dr. Angela B. Jones

Angela married Perry M. Jones. They have five children, seventeen Grandchildren, five great-grandchildren, and three daughter-in-loves. She is a retired military wife and has traveled to Germany, Panama, and Africa.

She received her Bachelor of Arts degree from Christopher Newport University, Newport News, Virginia, a Master of Arts Degree in Elementary Education at Hampton University in 1998, a Master of Divinity Degree in Theology from Virginia Union University, Doctoral in Ministry from Norfolk Theological College and Seminary, Norfolk, VA.; while serving as an interim professor.

Angela is the founder of the Rose of Sharon Christian Ministries and the Ambassadors for Christ Summer Camp Outreach Ministry in Creswell, Roper, and Columbia, N.C., "His Banner Over Us Is Love" WGAI 360am. Radio Ministry broadcasting Saturdays from 10:15-10:30 am.

Isaiah 49:3 "And he said to me, you are my servant, Israel, in whom I will be glorified."

Connect with Angela at: abhumble52@yahoo.com

Charmaigne L. Lloyd

Charmaigne is a dedicated Middle School Math Teacher, Curriculum Writer, Academic Architect, and 7th Grade Team Lead with a passion for education since 1995. She teaches for Richmond Public Schools and is endorsed in PreK-6 Elementary Education, K-12 Special Education, 6-8 Middle School Math. Originally from Brooklyn, New York, Charmaigne is the proud mother of five beautiful children.

She has been recognized as the New Teacher of the Year in 2022 and Teacher of the Year 2024. Charmaigne earned her Associate's in Early Childhood Education (2002) and a Bachelor's in Education (2012), and is on track to complete her Master's in Reading and Literacy in June 2025. She believes in the transformative power of the butterfly effect, which is crucial for change in the lives of children and adults alike. Her philosophy is to "Foster self-discovery, embrace diversity, ensure equity, and empower children to thrive holistically.

Connect with Charmaigne at:
clloyd4hispurpose@gmail.com

Natasha Broughton

Natasha is the visionary and founder of Her Renewed Identity Coaching Services which serves women who are seeking to embrace their Identity in Christ without shame, shrinking or defeat. With Natasha's passion and love for children, she is dedicated to teaching children inside and outside of the classroom. Natasha is ready to walk fully in her purpose as a life-coach and mentor. Natasha is newly married and is the proud wife of Julian Broughton. Natasha is looking forward to helping women walk in their God-given identity and helping impact the lives of everyone she meets.

Connect with Natasha at: info@iamnatashamonique.com

Leona Elzy

Leona is a native of New Orleans, Louisiana. She is a mother of three and a United States Navy veteran. Leona has a passion for healthcare and began her career in the medical field while in high school. Upon receiving her high school diploma she was also certified as a Nursing Aide. She also served as a Hospital Corpsman before obtaining her undergraduate degree in science. She now works as a Clinical Functions Advisor. In addition, Leona faithfully serves on the Nursing ministry in her church. She began writing at an early age, loves to write poetry, and has one previously published poem. Leona is an avid reader and has a passion for sharing stories with others.

Connect with Leona at: Galmon.Elzy@gmail.com

Salesha LOL

Salesha LOL is a native of Portsmouth, VA, and is a proud graduate of I.C. Norcom High School where she earned her Advanced Studies Diploma. While in high school, Salesha completed an internship at a local Housing Authority where she developed a passion to assist others in becoming self-sufficient. Although she finished her education with a bachelor's degree in business management at Strayer University, she will always claim to be an NSU Spartan from her short time there. Her compassion for others increased during her seventeen-year career in the Housing Industry where she witnessed many of her tenants struggle to maintain stable housing. Being limited in how she could help as a landlord, she decided to switch seats at the table to assist the A.L.I.C.E. population in becoming financially stable by earning her HUD Housing Counselor and Credit Coach Certification. In her spare time, she likes to indulge in all things self-care, travel, music, and creating memories with her love, family, and friends.

Connect with Salesha at: https://linktr.ee/saleshalol

Michelle M. Hicks

Michelle is a Richmond, Virginia native and a dedicated leader in ministry. Licensed to preach in 2004 and ordained in 2012, she currently serves as Pastor of Christian Tabernacle in Petersburg VA where she preaches and serves with her husband Bishop Kenneth L. Hicks Sr. Michelle has held numerous roles in the church, including youth leader, women's ministry head, and intercessory prayer leader. She founded the Be My Sister for Real Conferences, a nationwide ministry focused on healing and empowerment, and Free To Be Me Ministries which teaches that it's the truth that makes you free to be who God created you to be. Michelle's passion is delivering messages of healing and deliverance through prophetic insight.

In addition to Pastor and now author, Michelle is Mom to five children, Granny to 17 grandchildren and 2 great-grandchildren, and Spiritual Mother to a host of others who affectionately seek her guidance and wisdom.

Connect with Michelle at: freetobemeministry@gmail.com

Zaquinntia "Zee" Chamblee

Zaquinntia "Zee" Chamblee was born and raised by a beautiful single mother in Atlanta, Georgia. She is a mother of a delightful adult daughter, a handsome adult son, and two adorable granddaughters. She is a full-time healthcare worker, Veteran Family liaison with Innovative Veteran Outreach. She earned her undergraduate degree in Human Services and is a full-time graduate student, in pursuit of her degree in Master of Science in Education, majoring in Counseling (MSED), and a Concentration in Clinical Mental Health Counseling. She plans to continue assisting those with barriers because of their mental health by utilizing her degree in the Behavioral Health field.

After retiring over 20 years from Master Barbering and Hairstyling/Shop Owner, Zaquinntia realized that God was preparing her for counseling after years of listening and assisting her clients with their life circumstances by sharing coping skills with Godly instruction. After years of running from her calling, she finally answered God's call and continues to help His children navigate through life in a healthy and safe course of action.

Connect with Zaquinntia at: zcham002@odu.edu

Renita D. Harris

An experienced HR professional specializing in Employee Relations, **Renita** brings a positive attitude and vibrant energy to every challenge. Based in Chesapeake, VA, she balances a fulfilling career with life as a dedicated mother of two daughters Rakeya and Destiny. Known for her self-motivation, reliability, and strong teamwork skills, she excels in creating supportive and productive work environments. Outside of work, Renita enjoys unwinding on the beach at sunset, and has a passion for singing and dancing. Her mature approach and hard work make her a valued asset both professionally and personally.

Connect with Renita at: 3-keyandes2@gmail.com

Princess Barnes

Princess was born and raised in Portsmouth, Virginia by her mother, along with her two brothers. She currently resides in Chesapeake, Virginia. Princess is a wife, mother, grandmother, entrepreneur, and a bestselling author of "We Won't Quit". She and her husband Rarsan Barnes have been married for fourteen years and they have a blended family of five amazing children - three girls and two boys - as well as two beautiful granddaughters.

Princess has a Bachelor of Science in Health Administration from the University of Phoenix and is the founder and CEO of several businesses. Two of her businesses serve the elderly, intellectually disabled, and disabled individuals, as she believes that no one should be left behind. She also has a coaching and consulting company called The Lotus Group, where she assists individuals with starting up, operating, and expanding their businesses.

She's a disabled army veteran who takes pride in and enjoys helping and serving others. When she's not working, she spends her free time reading, writing, traveling the world, and enjoying her family.

Connect with Princess at: princessbarnes1982@gmail.com

Milton Keynes UK
Ingram Content Group UK Ltd.
UKHW020054181024
449757UK00011B/624